This to That and Thus

Shearsman Library Vol. 21

Also by Joseph Donahue

Before Creation (1989)
Monitions of the Approach (1991)
World Well Broken (1995)
Terra Lucida (1998)
Terra Lucida XVI–XX (1999)
Incidental Eclipse (2003)
In This Paradise: Terra Lucida XXI–XL (2004)
Terra Lucida (2009, revised edition)
Dissolves: Terra Lucida IV-VIII (2012)
Dark Church: Terra Lucida IX-XII (2015)
Red Flash on a Black Field (2015)
Wind Maps I–VII (2018)
The Disappearance of Fate (2019)
Infinite Criteria (2022)
Terra Lucida XIII–XXI Música Callada & Near Star (2024)
Disfluency, Collected Uncollected Poems 1973–2023 (2024)

As editor

Primary Trouble: An Anthology of Contemporary American Poetry (1996; with Edward Foster and Leonard Schwartz)
The World in Time and Space: Towards a History of Innovative American Poetry in Our Time (2002; with Edward Foster)

This to That and Thus

Poems 1983–1998

Joseph Donahue

Shearsman Books

First published in the United Kingdom in 2025 by
Shearsman Books Ltd
PO Box 4239
Swindon
SN3 9FN

Shearsman Books Ltd Registered Office
30–31 St. James Place, Mangotsfield, Bristol BS16 9JB
(this address not for correspondence)

EU AUTHORISED REPRESENTATIVE:
Lightning Source France
1 Av. Johannes Gutenberg, 78310 Maurepas, France
Email: compliance@lightningsource.fr

ISBN 978-1-84861-983-8

Copyright © 2025 by Joseph Donahue.
The right of Joseph Donahue to be identified as the author of this
work has been asserted by him in accordance with the
Copyrights, Designs and Patents Act of 1988.
All rights reserved.

ACKNOWLEDGEMENTS
The books reprinted here originally appeared as follows:

Before Creation (Central Park Editions, New York, NY, 1989)
Monitions of the Approach (Red Dust, New York, NY, 1989)
World Well Broken (Talisman House Publishers, Jersey City, NJ, 1995)
Incidental Eclipse (Talisman House Publishers, Jersey City, NJ, 2003)

Some of the poems appeared in: *Acts, Alea, Central Park, Hambone, Notus, Talisman, Temblor, The Five Finger Review,* and *Ur Vox.*

CONTENTS

Before Creation	9
Guest Plus Host Equals Ghost	14
Errand Immanent	16
Misplaced Parrhesia	17
Lou Reed	18
Lenny Bruce	19
Such Nights As	22
Here and There	23
Open All Night	33
Crania Americana	40
Thunderclap	49
God's Blossom	50
A Curse Upon the Saintly Corpse of Luis Buñuel	51
Another Gala Evening	54
Posthaste and Romage	55
Desire	57
Monitions of the Approach	64
Opiate Phobia	81
The Wild Colonial Boy	82
The Age of Oracles	86
Spectral Evidence	89
Flash Cards	101
Christ Enters Manhattan	107
Incidental Eclipse	128
Area Elsewhere	132
Lost Letter in a Last Word	136
A Parish in the North	138
Parade Route	142
Scandalized Masks	145
For Edmund Spenser	148
The White Tomb	151
Neon in Daylight	153
Here / Beyond	155
Aria Nowhere	159

Occult Blood	163
Life Outside the Gutter Factory	165
Targets, Mongolia	168
This to That and Thus	170
All the While	173
Off the Map	176

"…this to that and thus…"
—William Bronk

Before Creation

for John Yau

I

Other lives, their jostle. The engineer
crumples error into a paper ball, hurls it
as I enter. Man in the locker room,
skeleton beneath pale ripples
of fleshless skin. Corner phone,
the acting vice president, her son
beaten with a pipe in a drug deal.
Girl in skintight purple. A red
sash, an elevator's closing door.
Hand on shoulder, wrong number.
Other lives, your own, partaken
of, or not. In a white coat lamenting
new difficulties. Delirious fruit,
eaten with odd effect. A corpse
upright on the median bench.
Bits of bodies blown over
the airwaves. A sky-blue eye,
clouded: a subway poster,
a swastika etched in the pupil.

II

Cruelties: Mayan priest, radio atheist,
but also: Constantinople's walls and towers.
A mind, done in by doctrine. A man
in a motorized wheelchair questioned
with concern by a woman in remission.
Blue pool: the dead man's pied-à-terre.
Days at work, the boss not in. What
Summa survives the saint who writes it?

Message in red, left on my desk.
Bible, a nail driven through it,
found where the convict took the girl.
The Grail. Fourfold method wrecked
by an envelope. Noble ghost, you call me.
Disparate myths: intertwined,
a glowing gospel. Days at work,
news of the suicide. Nothing done
but thoughts for the dead.

III

Misfiled at the precinct. A
clipping, a classmate's marriage,
mailed with bitter humor.
We went at it for hours.
None of the old problems.
Afterwards she slept, but I was
ecstatic. Newspaper cut, rolled
and tied in a handkerchief:
disaster followed when she
followed her conscience.
Mount Tabor in evening light,
a deity revealed, his prophets.
Woman in a blue dress.
Her lost contact lens.
A snapshot once carried
in a wallet found amid the
paper clips at the bottom
of a filing cabinet. The cop
wrote down what happened.
Handkerchief full of money.
On the mountaintop, with
John and James. Fiery visions
of spiritual bodies. Unspoken
cohesions. The data grows

urgent. The victim of the
swindle opens the handkerchief.
Down from the mountain, far
wall of the polis, to sleep by
an olive tree until dawn.
A last postcard after
they agreed not to write:
a table set with linen and silver.
Her entrance, nine years back.
Asked by police if a car
was involved. Driven by
misery to a shrink. You are
not the victim of a swindle.
Elijah, Christ and Moses,
etched in the pupil of an eye.

IV

Eye contact: refresher course
on asocial symptoms. Realizing
how you look in your coat with
stains from high school. Summoned
as a juror. A friend you give up on,
an adversary you honor. Colonial
attitude of the mind toward
its residence. She allows
you to undress her, in fact she
encourages you. Plum blossoms,
joys without repercussion.
Think of how you used to think.
Anger eases into languor. She leans
From the steam cloud, sips the cold beer
on the soap dish by the sink. A tally
of torments is not a full account.
Gold fleck: her eye: the flutter
preceding the mention of it.
Resented for my apartment's lobby:

had she lived here the attack
could not have happened.
Reddish tint: sunset on brick.
Cluster of Jews at ease on
the street. We have half
an hour to get to the florist or
the bouquet will be bolted in,
nightlight and alarm, and we
will arrive at the party
having failed our promise.

V

Days at work, message in red ink.
Phoned long-distance from a hospital bed.
But if I am still only a living ghost
how can I house the spirits of the dead?
Lavabo inter innocentes manus meas:
et circumdabo altare tuum, Domine.
Not that, but not uninformed of that.
Man draped in Nazi flag, naked, at a party.
Conversation with a puppeteer about
the spirit world. Dismal air quality,
can't keep my lenses in. Attached
to oxygen. Infection abated. The
children wear masks when they visit.
Lord our brother has been dead three days.
The kidnapper called the radio station
to request a song but then shot
himself before it came on. Sky the
color of tabloid print washed from
my hands, New York rinsed by rain.
Deep breath in the silence. Called
by a voice both my own and not.
Adolescence in Egypt, acolyte
to an idol. Black horizon of a
planet, a narcotic flower opens.

Dawn: unsettled dead, a riverbank.
I sift through manias, rigors, lapses.
I hunger to inhabit a living form.
On the laundromat floor the towel
that Pilate used. Golgotha. Sinai. Tabor.
Covered today by ash-colored clouds.

VI

All visible phenomena seemed
evidence in a vast and unpublished
criminal proceeding. Reprieve
of morning crucified by noon.
Updraft on the avenue. Paper bag
clearing the girders of the new high-rise.
Welder's spark, downward arc of slight fire.
(This, a manual for a ballistics expert.)
The jury clamors, no goddess descends.
Orestes is condemned to scrub the
blood from his parents' house.
Beside the boarded drugstore the
zealot lashes out at the
profligate teenagers. Podium:
a senator lamenting his past:
"Let Love gather my scattered limbs."
Horror deepening the hope.
In corrupt versions of the legend
gods applaud the murder. Sunlight.
Whitened steps. A skull twisted like
paraffin left on a hot stove. As I
unpack my lunch: tales of
a plastic surgeon on the
Amtrak to Boston. Disfigured,
restored, which is our true face?
Scales. Banquet hall of the dead.
Questions still to come from
the throne I stand before.

Guest Plus Host Equals Ghost

Trashfire
in a barrel,
gnosis. Or:

severed
hand, outside
the doughnut shop.

Or: a guest
you hesitate
to admit,

man with a
newspaper
you haven't read.

Hour-long wait
for an infusion
of blood,

lifelong wait
for a change
in mood.

The Pakistani
bows in prayer.
Red crest

floods Manhattan,
O gathering blaze
of Ramadan.

Girl I ushered
to the hospital
half dead

from false
devotion.
Afternoon in

the antique shop,
looking for the real
amid the replicas.

The brilliance
of the idol
fascinated

Moses, even
as he loathed it.
Bodies dug up,

*negligible
martyrs*. To find
an assertion

in an era
of disbelief.
To change,

after signing,
the contract.
Their deities came

to understand
them, picking the bones
of the worshippers,

ascending
as black
birds.

Errand Immanent

Silverbowl, bloodied rim: the moon. Radiant smoke pouring from heaven's gutter, night sky through which electrons beam documents of further holocaust.

In blue televised light let the builder rest, the actress find peace. But the singer, let him enter a darker continuum.

Is this the hour the soul flies from its house to rest in the arms of the Beloved?

Nights in New York. The murdered girl awoke. The theatre, wreckage and cloud. The gold harp smeared with her blood.

Six times sun and moon ignite the ocean's broken glitter.

She becomes a breeze blowing to the land of the dead. Branches, green, and a garden walled in stone. Her guard begins:

> Allow nothing but the violence you no longer feel.
> You can stay here, dwelling in thought.
> Nothing will restore you to life.

Misplaced Parrhesia

I am not brilliance come to bear away darkness in the night by speech alone, says client to therapist in a dream she won't remember. Ringing off the hook, the office deserted. Today there are other messages I want to write down. Sunlit game room. A laetrile clinic in Mexico. The government buys findings to strengthen its investments. No end to contention over method. No end to the agon of cure. Noble shade: jolt of a profile: not your widow, but close. Clouded bus, rain-soaked clothes. Blessedness, said William James, a fragile fiction. Each in the room told in turn the past as if it were over. Morning at the movies: the two rich college girls blew the gardener. On the street at night, despite all the clatter, you feel you are in the alcove of a chapel. When you can name the voices, you will know which one has your assent. The truer god does not die for you, but with you, was how the recent claim went. Two figures interlocked in the corridor of a welfare hotel. Film stars of the forties, embracing on a stage. The kiss: guilt, taken as contrition. Cloud: hem of Christ's garment. May it pass from the sky so that emptiness might heal the world. Dog-eared catechisms, jottings of anthropologists, recollections of childhood, ancestral ghosts, from other lives, their jostle. From a cloud, from a coffin, from a table set for guests. Less for the dead, more for what within one is dead. Clear blue blast between buildings. The plane cuts upward. Beneath the ocean, a constant fire. Life thrives in the lava where hell was.

Lou Reed

Teamsters in trucks wave blue and white streamers.
Desolate hoopla. Copper wire looped through
the ignition. Into the gas tank, and that's all.
A terrorist in a toy store, taken by
remote-control gizmos. Lou Reed steps
to the mike, begins "White Light/White Heat."
These monolithic theories of myth,
there's no stopping them. She kissed me
then dropped to her knees. I just want
to please you. That was 1978.
Kill Reagan, the shout rings out. Man with
the head of a computer terminal dances
with a svelte skeleton. Or angular,
in a black tux. The woman with a gold
pocketbook. Beg, lash. Beg, attack.
(The weak tell the truth, the strong
take up disguises.) Storm imminent,
lightning. Prairie awash in purple light.
1970. Pants patched with stars from a flag.
The vodka hypnotic, as were our conjectures.
Reading Nietzsche: the morality of sheep,
so virginal a concept. Inverted
feelings of national purpose: black
fighter planes hidden in a bare grove.
White light tickles me, right down to my toes.

Lenny Bruce

Maybe what I mean
by the State differs
from what you mean —

blood pulse, over stone.
Daughter or sacred deer
slain: a death to

break the heat spell.
Orange juice, sherbet.
The blender a sugar blast

in lieu of a drink.
Alas! Hauteur with which you greet
your unemployment:

I have become a god!
Chide of a man from the
Coroner's Office:

*more prints than on
Governor Carey's wife's ass.*
(White House pix in

a black pianist's hands.)
When Reagan calls on
his First Counselor

he means Christ.
Rodents in rubbish,
Lux fiat.

Dead water, slack sail.
The glories of South America
must await further plunder

until the apocalypse
becomes our
household routine.

*I had a twin and
my hunger killed her.*
The proxy vote from

Purgatory, said Lenny Bruce,
has yet to be counted.
Skydiver dead in the Carolinas —

a waste of so much
cocaine. The audience
chanted *Kill her.*

Kill Iphigenia,
though this was no
1930s Hoboken bund rally.

So, Moses turns Pharaoh,
Antigone, Creon. Each bound
unto annihilation, unto

5 o'clock. Glitter
of river, pulse of bridge,
infant lifted to lights

of a far shore.
Take thine only son.
"Physiological. Must be.

You can see it. He
changes. The new place
has attendants and he's scared —

manipulating the hell
out of me.) *Take thine
only son, whom thou lovest.*

"He'll put my arse
to the fire this week
I can tell you, my arse

to the fire this week.
A terror comes over him,
Darvon's useless.

Pray. What can
you do just
pray."

Such Nights As

A blue silk scarf falls through the air.
Evening unmoors, undone by a current
that swept past Mexico two days back.

Jungle colors: exuberant fauna
in the void where the temple stood.
Her leather jacket, pulled tight.

She tells of a closet: a single priceless
dress embroidered with stories. She
has never felt loved enough to wear it.

The avenue mirrors the sky.
Fireworks illumine the hospital
and sear the gold reed in the angel's hand:

not yet, not yet. Lesser nights are
still in rehearsal. The corporal's torn sleeve,
the duenna's frill, are unfathomed.

The librarian has locked the door
and left the electric globe switched on.
Red and gold continents drift through

iridescent latitudes: a mind
free of need. Or perhaps a need
free at last to enter the mind —

messages flicker. Names on a tape.
Packet of cocaine taped onto a mirror,
lost in the red tumult of her hair.

Lavish absence. Translucent street,
entrance of pearl. Not yet, not yet.
A blue silk scarf falls through the air.

Here and There

I

I'm poison, she remarked. Hands lost
in a clutch of fresh basil. Tiles
vivid in the bath where she soothes herself.
Undulations of color, float of her touch.

Deck above breakwater. Sunset a
conch amid the darkening splendors.
Mahogany stern, name in gold script:
Shuttle of Spirits.

        That, and a
tasteless remark by a French gynecologist
on a fishing boat bound for Brooklyn.
Chivalric age, where gulls dive
for bottlecaps. Memphis to Mobile,
Mycenae to Montauk.

                Black tangle
of her bathing suit as she stepped from it.
Later, the living legend steps to the mike
and begins *A Night in Tunisia.*
    Her subsequent dream: a white horse,
    a damaged hand (her father a surgeon).

Branches flutter,
handmaiden and trees.
I wash in a stream. In green water.
And then begin to tell my tale:

    (In *another life,*
        I was J.F.K.
                Cavalcade of
state-regulated hero cults. The

slain brothers stalk
the convention.)

           Shuttle
of starlight. The beach at night. Grasses bend.
She lies down. On her back. On
top of him. So they both can gaze
into the sprawl of stars?

Thought and desire:
                      a rational fire.

Tremble of grass blades,
    hornets lace through them,
        rest in the gold curl of leaves.
First updraft of autumn. Floral skirt.
Swirl of petals in a green field.

The labor that the soul
    desires, and the labor that
        the body demands.

The Beethoven of bebop steps to the mike,
begins *In the Land of Milk and Honey*.
Carolina to Cairo. What fills
my head when the radio's off?
Colors of fear and adoration.
The motif, intrusion.
    The glance, amorous.

Inkblue sea and fiery sky
    as seen from a fisherman's bar.
Pale green liqueur against violet striations.
Water reflecting the sky reflecting the sun.
Thought and desire,
                horizon of fire.

The lovers begin to deceive each other.

II

Arguments prompt the particulars,
themselves the result of other arguments,
utterly forgotten.

    A friend you run into changing trains
    who saw her at a Xerox machine in
    Charlottesville. A year and a half ago.

Balcony above the courtyard,
the quartet at night. That, and the
hashish smoked with the other Americans.

    Here and there. Ten years and now.
    His analyst suggested he look at his hands
    and notice where his attention drifted.

    *   *   *

And if you're not scared 60%
of the time you're not alive,
the lawyer said.
              Hailstones.
Runway blackened with rain.
At mid-cabin we have Tina
and Dan. Theories of
cultural change. That was not
what swept over him, there
beside the duckpond.
Phantom billow of rain.
What he was a part of
seemed to him only a slight part
of what he was.

        Orange clouds
scratched in a purple sky,
the partial vision of the living.

    Mural whitewashed, the commercial shot.
    "Gets himself a mule who peddles it for him."
    And that other 40%, how shall I fill it?

Tuft of cloud, gold.
Blue cloud, smoky.
The rim of the earth
a stripe of fire.

Relentless conviction:
that I can see beyond it.

*Swing low
sweet Cadillac.*

    Back in New York the question
    each fought to contain was: how to
    adapt Dostoevsky to the stage.

Chemise, violet silk.
Bright skirt and sandals,
a Spanish perfume.
A mysticism of positions,
she remarked.
White wine in a clear cup.
Lustre, of gold,
of polished wood.
(Trumpet and tambourine.)
White tentflaps taper
down to the lawn,
balloon a solar bark
above the sea's motion —

"Dumdum bullets. Very illegal.
I got him to open the briefcase. I'd
never been in the presence of so much cash."

*the god entered me
and my wounds vanished.*

*   *   *

Mussel-blue ocean, chill deck.
They sipped the sauce from
empty shells. Multicolored
pennants in the wind.
Haiti in December? They
could just manage it.
Anticipation disconnected
from the excitement. Not
the smooth beaches and
turquoise depths, but that
time had entered, at last,
their conversation.

III

"This and other
    perplexities
confront the inquirer into
    the origin of heroic
personalities."

        Desire,
utterly gave up on it and now
all these women want to sleep with me,
so he confided, back, with a tan,
from Venice.

    Red and yellow
    configurations: god and goddess
    procreate, limbs wreathed, tongues twined,
    eyes not quite closed. What does the
    queen weave into her robe?

The speeding cars spin out,
one into the parked cars on the far side,
the other crosses lanes.
Air hammers, billows of white smoke.
Joggers stop, myself among them.

Black rubber sleeve,
yellow band. The IV bottle
floats above the heads of the crowd.
I continue to circle the block.

> *I'm not angry it*
> *takes more than what*
> *we had for me to*
> *fall in love.*
> Eerie, the
> effect of the neon
> restaurant sign
> on her diaphanous
> blouse, on the creamy tan
> of her neck and face.

I continue to circle the block.
T-shirt, clinging with sweat.
These are the bones of the body,
the body that was Jesus.
Around the block,
burgundy-colored
silk gowns, a bride
in sunlight.

IV

Clouds enclose Manhattan.
    Rises from white shimmer

the first of the visions which solitude can promise.

The power of a swimmer in green water.
    A dream of confidence
        after great duress
in which you are shown
    a beautiful house
        by the daughter of a dead man.

To gain control
over the axe which
caused the wound
chant the myth
of the origin
of iron,

        of almond-
scented coffee
in a blue cup.
The Song of Songs
is the holiest of texts
remarked the rabbi
turned activist.
But Cajun blues played
on an accordion,
these too are among the
sanctities.

Her belt, red. With metal studs.
Late. Near four. The ghost
of her sister passed through her.
(The thinness of a friend's wife brought it all back.)

Clouds enclose Manhattan.
    Rises from white shimmer

excitement. Streamers and
roped-off side streets. Scent
of roasted meat and mingling spices.
Ideas at last at one with details —

    Every product has
    an inherent drama,
    said Leo Burnett. The
    Marlboro Man. Hell,
    Tony the Tiger. These
    are masterpieces.

But the iron mask of the actor alters the comedy.

Spate of days, each
more languid, more celibate.
As if all that desiccation were
    an orchestral chafe.

First breath,
Genesis.

    I opened up.
I told you things,
Call me.

V

The evidence baffled the fledgling attorney.
He sifts the welter, in search of the concealed idea.

As if the crime
was a vindication.

As if the indigo
wash of evening
altered each fact.
As if the ghost of
Wallace Stevens had
anything to tell me,
here in my red chair,
overlooking the
empty street.

    Blue blanket, gold stars, the
    enraptured goddess tilts her head back,
    her shoulders turned from the foreground.
    Figures grace the grove. Some watch
    the divinities fuck, but not all.

Spicy billows of steam,
fresh soup in the apartment below.
Copper pot, bowl, bread on a blue plate.
The meat succulent, and the broth.
Red, green, vegetables swirl to the surface.

The hallway fills with ideas
    of propitiation and appetite
        and autumn drizzle.

The ritual a composite of
    other rituals. At the center
        a deity without hands or eyes.

Their affair transfigured the thought of autumn.
Blue Camaro, there as the train pulls in,
the sky raddled pink and orange and deepest blue.

    "Intellectualizers react to
    the figure, while hysteroids
    are capsized by sudden color."

The severed head
of a sow lands at
my feet and the
bridesmaid tells me:
*that roll of film
you wanted is
inside it.*

Open All Night

I

Lordly months
and very low clouds.

Across the river did you hear?
A father killed his son with a nail

a hammer
and a blanket.

*Yes yes it's coming
to an end. All of it.*

An alliance eclipsed by a single orgasm.
(Bodies both dust now.)

Emanation, abyss.
Warship lashed to a phonebooth

and friends
five years gone.

The plane's black box hidden in the blaze.
Across the river Omega

carved in
fuselage and brick.

Arm caught at a crosswalk,
a novel's worth of narrative.

Shotgun looped to a clown's head.
Welcome the electricity of human thought!

said Dostoevsky.
Blue pool, cluster of green.

What keeps me from the Creation?
The river's rippling flame and

Anger, unveiled.
As implement. As coercion.

As a needlemark
worth noting.

II

Festivities at the sound truck.
The slain man jumps up and hits his mark again.

Turned down as
a donor: a cancerous past.

Nostalgia
for Manson,

murderer as exegete.
Six flights above the muck.

Wingbeat: her breath against his cock.
(All jokes begin in prison.)

Terminal smoke unfolds,
transvestite fanning herself with a torn phone bill.

Elderly man in whose soup the plaster fell
shrieking at the subcontractor.

Without the lens
there's no myopia.

Six flights above the muck
with the attitude of an outpatient.

He told me he'd been
an actor in *Scorpio Rising*.

Both my ankles were broken.
I was bleeding from places quite remarkable.

Apocalypse,
garden. Enough

of one for a down
payment on the other.

Airshaft: whirlwind of snow.
Even here some purity reaches me.

III

Angelic
flicker in fiery script,

in dawn's delicate white smoke
and the green plume of an African prince.

Each to the other
a knockout dose

wrapped in a cancelled check.
In some alternate cosmos

curses are sewn into the mouth of a toad.
What pierces the shimmer of time's empire?

*Whenever
you feel noble*

remember, she said,
it's because of your hatred.

The train pulls in and boredom lifts.
I wake from centuries of sleep and pull back the curtain.

Barbaric
dancers in leather briefs.

Her tan made her seem Hispanic.
Conversation about a new flotation tank

adrift in living death.
In some alternate cosmos

a slate engraved with violations loops my neck.
Cold stream where the groom swam naked

erased
by orange moonlight.

*I'm not
resisting…*

*But you want to?…
Yes…*

IV

Their lawyers tell me
what a good eunuch I am.

And from Cairo?
A necropolitical calm.

Robed in black her rival jokes:
my blood's in steel tubs

at the hospital.
And Mr. Castellano?

Dining in eternity's steakhouse...
Drawer dumped out and the clock gone,

apotheosis
of venal deities.

Eyeball excised
then the screwup:

formaldehyde in the spine.
Dave talked to the Disney people.

Is it worth our while to meet with them?
Open all night the whole

audible world, looters
knocking the wounded in haste

to rob the dead.
Snowfall, coffin factory.

Words once mystical are now almost viral.
Walls white, receptionist svelte.

My moral inferior. I hated that man
and held his hand as he died.

Remember: the wrong
ejaculation in the wrong

jar's
pointless.

V

Home from the sound studio:
Lake water. Bicycle wheel. Heat pipe.

Snow crust underfoot. Subvocal
articulations. Shatter of

a rearview mirror when
the ambulance gets clipped

by a film production van.
All things are most what they are

when they say they are not, —
The cheekbone's plastic

but the pancake hides it.
Tension brings on the infection

and I feel inadequate.
Hands lashed; bodies dumped on a ramp.

Having exhausted the supply
of Israeli girls they begin

to execute Americans.
Terrorists from South Terannia

attack the rock star.
The proceeds from her master tape

will feed the starving in North Terannia.
Red beep. Alarm light. Panic. Plunge.

Rooftop vertigo, her voice and
with each step the sound of breakage.

Sky tilting green to black —
Schizotypic. And amid

the dissonance, the summit
conference of saxophone and flute:

That's not a hotel.
It's where the poor die.

Crania Americana

for Albert Mobilio

Each day a stair in a staircase. Unruly bundle
on my back. A fiery sun I nail to the sky's beam.
The sticks of love and hate burning to ash at
the center of my task are not mine. Perhaps
under some other sky some other slave twists
beneath an unruly bundle, a fiery sun consuming
my woe. He also hates the hand that set it burning.

I

What grandeur of what damage
antedating time still reaches me?
Mingus steps up to the mike
and removes himself from the Powell debacle.
Corridor quick with violent color.
Temporal lesion: I near a place where
voice gets severed from the body.
Get a Sony microtape, the novelist said,
let nothing escape. Lonelier
than God before the Creation.
That was the effect the cameraman wanted
on this, the rock star's first beer commercial.
Hands tarred, the slave awakes.
The master will know
who climbed the fence around the garden.
Vulvic lesion, image stream.
I wait behind the paper wall to join
my one vowel to the dolorous and ecstatic moan.
It was like infinity. She liked it too.
Be sure to wash yourself off after.
His dreams were sad because they were true.
Her dreams were sad because they were not true.
Galaxy, condom spatter.

Starry cast of a numinous sot.
(Truth a relation, he said,
of speaker and sentence and time.)
Banished from all mana the dead slave
and the living slave are one.
The infection must have come from you.
The music hides behind the silence
and hates the instrument that calls it forth.

II

A gasp,
a whirlwind
invigorating the
airshaft,
the syllabic
ditch.
Behind many,
a single voice.
And behind that?
Spurt and jibe
and coax,
the audible
contour
of the earth,
what Whitman said
shall *justify*…
Night. Quiet
consuming the words
that proclaim it.
Shrieks bristle
the gab.

III

The smoke starts here and winds up there.
I develop what other people shoot.
Desire defaced by its objects,
objects obliterated by their properties.
Face flush. Streaming in a cool room.
Take one of these. Turns
a sunny day into a dark night.
Zeitgeist, a punctured beach ball.
I near a place where voice enslaves the body.
The prop requires a last splash of red.
Grandad's ashes? I left them at the office.
Child clutching a plastic dinosaur an heir of
postwar Korean pharmaceuticals. Or: an actress
sprung from an Oklahoma war bride.
Last name? They traced it.
Back in Italy we cut off heads.
Crania Americana.
Descend this ladder of skulls,
Fiery Lord. Hammer this dagger.
Part writes the words and part stands aghast.
Himmler swapped my grandfather to the Swiss,
one in a boatload Roosevelt turned back.
(The icon's been moved. Mother's furious.)
The further from Creation
the greater the violence needed.
O make these things holy.
Clouds before dawn, green and purple.
The first slave sets foot in the New World.
Hands tarred from the fence around the garden.
I dream a banquet of pure chant.
I walk toward gunfire,
behind that dream is another.
As the melancholic hides behind his dolor,
as the word *fiend* hides behind the word *friend*.
The gate flames open. Thel flies.

Digression in a pulp mag: O Texas,
O natal state transfigured
by the invention of barbed wire.
History's oratorio across the corridor,
a psychosurgical impromptu. Voice
broken to bits and scattered she said
if she were a man she'd marry me in a minute.
The fake body tumbles four flights
bursting into sawdust. My voice
continues, though I am struck dumb.
They paint the staircase then refilm the murder.
I walk amid the poor at night.
Houses burning, shouts from the river.
I wanted to tell you,
but even in the dream I knew you were dead.
Orgasms flicker and the war breeds.
Jostle. Unutterable apothems.
Behind each word said
a word which cannot be said.
Abnegation upholding all things.
Axes glance each phase of Creation.

IV

Glorious
immortals bled
the world. Stone
snowed over,
roses lay on ice.
Police spray the room.
Meanwhile language tapes and
medical forms smoke
in a trash bin.
Collared monkeys
chatter scripts of terror.
(The patron has chosen his meal.)

Iranians hasten their mock executions
as ice-skaters sweep the rink.
Cleft of her love
delicately evident through
dirty sweatpants.
Noble ghost,
I pick up a ringing phone.
Does the silence confirm that I speak for you?
Genitals pierced with a stingray's tail.
The shriek God's
recompense for Creation.
Kingly blood in clay bowls
and groomed as I am to
hallucinate.
Drugs or bodily fluid turn the floor blue.
Woman stepping into a tub of dye.
Identities all broken.
No genealogy but speech.
Soaked paper
smeared on idols
burned in tribute's bowl.
Home a syllable hidden in a land
of kings and slaves.
I dreamed you
cried out
Reach me.
Free me from this.

V

Wave's punch.
Day's haul drying on a flat rock.
The first fishing shack now a toolshed.
Coastal marsh a weedy road with thickets and
illegible headstones above a few dozen skulls.
Maine coast,

bright islands of Olson's call.
Incursions of the tribal in the meandering chat,
the jogger and his future sister-in-law.
Gold flame. River of sun. Icy crust
and quiet after nights of restlessness.
Home no longer a place but the breath venting the word.
Gold watch reflecting
the sun above the river onto the page.
I live in grief, desiring you.
Steam, fever, nights apart, barely able to stand,
she slips into a slinky black thing
Just so you don't forget.
Adagios of appetite and silence,
thin strap of a flowered top torn from your shoulder.
House in the forest. Grass. Heaven's prairie
and light unravelling through me.
Seldom adrift on it, but now.
(Someone wants to take my happiness from me.)
No emblematic animals with starry pelts.
No caged man with eyes the crows pick clean.
House in deepening forest.
In the mix of syllables who utters the division of *love*?
Let Dante lament the gradations of Paradise.
Ripples of green wave through winter trees,
over white stones,
over the bones of Prince Edward,
Vanderveer's slave, drifting beneath a road
in suburban New Jersey,
whose spirit fled into Hegel's pen.
Animate chattel driven from sleep's forest.
Nothing I can choose that hasn't chosen me.
And when words move me,
what is the stillness through which
I feel the heart's motion?
Slaves gather. A field at night.
They crouch and pray. Blankets hanging
wet from low branches blot all sound.

And are there shiftings in the regions of water?
Are the beasts at ease in their procession?
Are the rivers rushing to one end?
Sun rolls over water. Almost reaches.
Like a bride who never arrives.
Each letter of her name lies hidden.
Like sap hidden in the delicate waver of a stem.
Like slaves hidden in the world's work.
Days, breaking emblems into gold dust.
Nights, gilding a prison.

VI

Effluvium of stars and fuel scent.
July night. Bodies tremble in a tangle
of laundry. Rooftop a green
combustible welter, meat chunks
on hooks, no voice, no Blakean flames.
Just aluminum-colored crab and rotten mango,
a skinned goat lolling over the butcher's white shoulder.
Haze over Manhattan. Fiery pits
and dump trucks. The jurors discuss the crime.
July night. The *Watchtower* peers out.
Its digital clock floats over the Navy yard
and rides a river of oil,
the red numerals do not ignite.
Moon's barge, Bellevue. Memory of
a sleeve ruffled beneath a crush.
Her hand's last spasm, the train idle.
The crowd agape at the soul's leap into time.
Times Square waiter, his arm broken.
Man in a tropical shirt who does Nielsen ratings.
I am the alternate. I am not permitted to speak.
Sunrise, toxic newsflash.
A minor mass grave unearthed out west.
Intention and end are one, the coroner cries.

The lawyer observes the dead are black.
Act of God shattering all contract:
The Doctrine of Impossibility.
Haze over Manhattan. Fiery pits
and dump trucks. Voices flicker as
questions consume all context.
Red hours broken on the river's glide.
Near Crane's bridge but the sublet had no view.
Memory of Mojave dolor.
Coppery strata and mineral bins,
Jesus streaming through the car radio.
Night sky, pulse of Sputnik over the lake bed.
Slither of vermin, jism of Christ.
O autoerotic suicide…
Starry effluvium, green to black.
The convict looked back and saw his body
on the far shore. Smoked. Made jokes.
What happens in secret reaches the demons.
(An actor walks toward you across a red floor.)
Images, dancers, each wall a screen.
Guitarist torturing the guitar with
recollections of Hendrix.
What fuels the burning earth?
Martyrs and fetish dolls.

VII

In the world
of apparent causes
their torn chunks will make them holy.
Xenoglossia,
heart's gibberish.
Babo's head
throttled with thought
agape on a pike across the bright plaza.
Sun's pulse unraveling the river.

The vision came
and found the body cold.
Dreamless night.
Flicker, whip,
your cruelest word.
In the world of apparent causes
objects pursue
a manifold martyrdom.
(This cup. This table. This book.)
Disclosure, lush field.
I walk there calling spirits from the air.
Flashlight aimed at the heart of the forest.
Does a god live there?
Headsman
and priest are pillars of the state
wrote a witness of the Terror.
As are dwindling love
and deepening solitudes.
Orestes severs a finger for Apollo.
Dissuade
my hand from my arm.
Dissuade my breath
from another's frozen lips.

Thunderclap

The rain neither an arrest nor
a release. Froth of absent ocean.
No boat bears me, only infinite depth.
Ajax moves across a field. The god
strengthens his arm. His shield
gold with glory. Hailstones in blank heat.
Man with a naked doll astride his television.
Sky a violent corridor rippling light.
Water in the water tower trembles,
a vehement legend coincides with its hour.
From cloudy mansions they turn and wave —
The Five Fighting Sullivans.
There are two kinds, said Albert.
Those that hit the earth and those
that detonate a few hundred feet above.
Exuberant and mortal wound,
helpless in my rental suit and name tag.
The holiest text lofted above a troop train,
you know I'm being honest by the way I create
the semblance of honesty. Screams
and moans were coming from the pit.
One soul stood off, angry still.
Ajax moves across the field. The blue
sea trembles. Heads of cattle strung in a tent.
He cannot believe he is not killing the fathers.
Red curtains part, a woman looks out.
Scent of wetness as imagined by a galley slave
in the sun's fiery warship.

God's Blossom

Even the zoo closes
and Goebbels himself shows signs of the strain.
Chars don't lie. Fire burns up and out.
I spent the summer in a school for arson detection.
There's so much to learn.
Given to quickness
and spoils, the sword still wet.
Athene said: I can darken the most brilliant vision.
Woman with a pocketbook and blue lipstick,
man in a dark suit.
They slash at a glance the face of the victim.
Ecstatic moans in the airshaft.
The sergeant was an antisemite
and even he was shaken.
Sand and bracken tremble.
Hector's gift,
buried to the hilt.
The Aegean? I've never seen it.
Puff of sun. Fiery haze of no dawn.
I drift amid the smoking pyres of Berlin.
The armor of Achilles pitched in a river rife with pitch.
No need to provide for those left over.
Pine knot:
God's blossom
in the grain of the
coffin.

A Curse Upon the Saintly Corpse of Luis Buñuel

Once beheaded
the actress will
invigorate the cult

and again I'm
reading Catholic
mysticism, —

pentagrams lime
the lawns of Utah.
Dam's blue cusp

athrottle with fish.
Intuition
dwindles into

fact, milky wash
of toxin clouding
the river's field.

The pen a nail
in my hand. When you
think of the world,

said Swift,
give it a lash.
The medicine botched

and the landscape
volcanic. *I love
neurology.*

The seizures.
Killer star a thimble
of astral slime,

this and other
catastrophic laws.
You wake screaming

and beat the air conditioner.
All events a braid,
a sad mother's stitch.

The lesions on the feet
of a helpless racist
who once worked the Exchange.

(Here where no
love reaches, blank
page, you shimmer.)

Head of Sally
on the body of Sue
speaking senseless

words from the deep past.
Dawn pours from its thermos
orange cloud and

pale yellow sky.
Men are credible,
the man noted,

in accord with their evil.
All events a braid,
angry Hera's stitch.

Moonlight's stripe
paints the lake.
A winged cross

crawls from my side.
Ghost years gone
you are as you were.

I can feel it. You
walk the earth again.
Dream, a feast.

The waking world
an empty plate. The cult
mourns the priestess,

confidante
of generals. Her body
an altar each priest

defiles, as if to
inseminate death.
Hector trembles.

His strength assures
the ruin of his people.
A monk in white

abject before an icon.
In the distance
a woman strips, the

picnic's hilarity builds.
I keep reading books of
erotic degradation.

Another Gala Evening

To move among the arrivistes,
darkly festooned. To cross Death Valley in winter
O my Jerusalem, my Vegas. Green leaves of a passport.

Her recollections of Russia, circa 1961.
Of the tug of the clip that held her hair in place.
Of wild leopard asleep in a thicket.

Of petals held by communicants in Spain.
The scent of sea air comes over the desert.
The lonely soldier awakes. While he slept

the train crossed a continent. He was
in the habit of reducing the whole to a part
and mistaking the part for the whole

but afternoon gloom gives way to night.
Like a postcard from a friend who writes of a land
that only patience can make rise from the sea.

Gala evenings at the nation's capital.
When the knock comes, always answer alone.
You'll be gunned down but the rest will be spared.

Pearl-colored sash. The trees around the
glassed-in dance floor coiled with party lights,
snowy glaze of the ground the glint of her jewels.

Excuse me. I've got to spread some rumors…
Amid so many voices the voice of God directs you
to keep quiet, to transcribe their voices.

Posthaste and Romage

Sky,
broken into zones.
Half ecstatic transfiguration
and half resembling an agony without hope.
A frantic man in a work shirt tearing a sugar packet
who wants to write for television.
Apparently, Sabrina's had a nervous breakdown!
A woman stepping from the shower who takes
the curtain's white flicker for her towel.
Blue cup: each twist of steam
a naked outline. Branches wet, torn.
World Trade lost in the silver ball of a storm cloud.
You look up from your desk. You spiral free from
a recurrent daydream about an incident of self-blinding.
Neon coffee drops pouring from the billboard into the river.
The islands rising are drops of blood
scattered by a god's sword.
This, and other myths of pure origin.
Black robe of a Zen priest.
Sometimes I forget how to fold it
but my hands do it for me.
Blue fog. A bridge
the color of mountains upriver.
A friend calls the rain adoration.
River, white. Gold sky flaking into black.
Masquerade deepening the bonds.
But you are older and have begun to bathe
in the streams of light in which all things are named.
Brightness flows through the morning's wet field.
The branches in their green froth glisten and are not
indifferent to their own endurance.
Moods breed and climb in the wavering tone.
Fire escape. The gust dampens your face.
Friends are arriving with gifts for you.
The guide presses the arteries of a dying man.

Great murals on the wall of the next life blind the soul
with mountains, orchards, a path into white mist.
Kept from climbing the stair by suddenness,
all volition lost in her lashes. Thoughts rise
when all is falling, thinks the soggy jogger in red togs.
They dance around a guilty kiss
and she is gone, like svelte Death in Cocteau.
I can't explain where this joy is coming from.
Red robe lost in smoke and choruses,
a woman standing in a circle of fire.
A garden scratched in stone.
A flayed satyr cradling a child
as each cradles a fresh sentiment.
At midnight, rearrange the
letters until a rapture arises.

Desire

Death's green
and gold corona
in the wavering branch

& the shuttle of syllables through the white light
& the pleasure of the mind of God permeating all accident
& no, the guard cannot

shut the light from your cell.
The chasm of gold, spill of red on the river.
The black boat at midpoint and the island lifted in fire

or the incarnation
of color in a vivid field where
solitude opens toward you.

Not memory,
but its plenitude.
You awake from a joy

that trembles at the far end of time
unable to say what words have kissed you
in your sleep.

Day's ferocity meanders
through the lack of significant feeling
(Each watching

the face of the other fading,
each a ghost in the other's dream but only one is still alive)
& your thoughts circle back to Juan de la Cruz

his grimy dungeon when
tears still in evidence a woman steps from the shadow
of the psychiatrist's door giving you her number

& the prelude to an evening's
harmonic diaspora unrelated to
recent dark events.

Words freshly tilted drift askew.
The aura of recent racial beatings touches the airy realm of the
fire escape where she talks about her diffidence

about the man she's "with"
& the city arrests its nightly glimmer
to attend her vulnerability & the rain mingles with

your discreet elation as
continuities in the lives of others rise
like land seen from an approaching ship

but then the ship veers into choppier regions.
You feel upbraided by the pettiness of your agonies
though you are older than you look & edging into a crisis

which seems both intermittent & perpetual
& partakes of the more sinister
of rationales regarding the presence of the poor

who loll drugged
in broken boxes in icy weather as
further questions stir.

Desire a city across the water
which the attrition of leaves makes visible
or a time when place was simply

the notation of silence as
through smoke and rain
millennia exfoliate.

It's someone else's dream
this bewildered amusement left on your tape
this surprise party the world has arranged for you

life passes you wait for the secret call
when the guests have arrived, you wait for
the one who will intimately mislead you through the rain.

Yes, things seem to be happening
but far off and illegible like the bottom line of an eye chart.
You're frustrated in your search for some collapse of clarity

or deletion sufficient to break your
ritualized gestures of defeat, the way a sudden turn
toward intimacy in a conversation can resemble

a cycle of fire purifying your past.
But can you say what presses for entrance at the stern gate?
Now and then, there is a flicker at the edge of things

cancelling all disappointment
lifting you in the wave of others en route to work
as the world opens into amplitude & rushes into stillness.

You have lived in the expectation
of some startling recompense, like some secret
Spanish Jew enduring the Reformation you have tended

this law in silence, amid adversity.
Meaninglessness was simply a mood which bothered you
but now you shiver in this chaste defilement,

this voluptuous schism revitalizing all thought.
What was that shadow that flashed across the street?
Not a cloud, the living nightmare of a life, gone

as gold cataracts of light wash over the brick
braided & intricate as the portico of a Caribbean mosque.
There is no place you can enter and be safe at last.

Not even the raptures and hierarchies of art
or the luminous swath of rainclouds & blue mist
& the gold rooftop across the river

or the clusters of berries,
bare branch supple with raindrops
as the three sparrows rest and their weight does not

jostle the silver equipoise
of fallen rain tapering now
into exhilaration.

At night the letters
recombine in hopeful bulletins.
Not promises, but the pleasure they give.

Flare or flashbulb as the speaker reviews
abuses of a far-off prison system,
her turban the color of early spring

yellow inside fresh shoots breaking into cold wetness.
As if you had torn up a snapshot of some
remembered bliss —

Kodachrome bits blow through the world.
Incidents take on the color of that former time
though far from where you are.

Or as when the memory
of someone long dead brushes the mind —
You feel you have just seen a crucial part

of a life you can never know.
Where was that mountain town?
Why did the bare-breasted occultist warn you so cryptically?

Why did you steal a car
& who was the man who died in the parlor
with such violent bravura?

An embarkation has long been underway.
(You dream of your brother. You miss him.
He comes in, he's late for work, but he wants to ask you

if you will give him a swimming lesson.)
Your routine opens onto a sphere
colored with blankness & depth & beasts

from the scrolls of Renaissance cosmographers
& you discover that paralysis is part of the voyage
those twilit Sunday afternoons when phone rates are down

reconstructing daylight as night deepens.
Music cleansed of lament and
lutes & loved ones locked in earth

as from vast regions
facts reveal an altered emptiness
& you sense a desire behind desire & to taste that

would be to know
the beauty God knew
the moment before Creation

when meanings mirrored
the need which evinced them.
No view of the river today

its threads of green and gold.
The man in the cell
turns beneath his ratty blanket.

He is a second
Jean Genet, equally
stroked and scolded

but destroying his books so that
his lovers can never be distracted from his whims
by the beauty of their image in the text.

———————

All things announce the hour
the plane's shadow cutting the cloudbank
ocean the fiery

splay of noon's winter mirror.
The cities of the earth glitter in the folds of mountains
and yes, these dreams at last will lead you out of

famine and bondage.
You have no clear account of your route
except that a mystery sufficient to your desire

for comprehension awaits you.
Boat a fiery sliver toward what sea
its bowline script half risen from the froth

in the flux of inference adrift
in the echo of similitude across great distance
as in a notebook kept hidden for years & almost filled

silver threads the
interweaving current
broken

by a black branch
held in a window that looks onto brick.
You cannot see, but you see.

You do not
feel at home, but
you are.

Monitions of the Approach

As some anxiety with
intermittent luster freshens the stillness.
Like a woman who says I have a terrible headache

& was up for an hour
but then: in sleep I'm euphoric.
Mixture of sunlight & shade on the water.

Morning mist, a white screen.
Shadow of boats on the far side of the visible.
Immanent script, bowline & mast. Light finds you.

What seemed an agony
is the onset of a larger attentiveness.
Weeks pass, with their density & pressure

their reticent future —
flooding & falling back from
what shore.

———————

A boat in evening's opal.
Drinks, & a floating dance floor.
What onrush were you about to taste

what starry mayhem
through the deepest of the
season's poisons? —

A green coast propelling you.
Some fresh intelligence or origin
pouring through you —

as if your mother were not a singer
but song itself, your father not a lawyer
but law itself, & your torment

were born only
to correct your err-
oneous love…

As if no new matter's come
into Creation since the beginning —
that first ecstasy

guiding your steps
so elemental
& mortal.

———————

All's intimation, some
future intoxicant, & even in exile
Ovid ruled the regency of erotic tumult.

Useless hours flare in an unwritten book —
& dreams: not clear ones, they win their reward here,
but those obliterated save for one color or phrase.

Our death & birth are
flickers of shadow & light there, are motions of water.
Our earthly form, a few fiery words.

———————

Meanwhile: a secret's out.
Love's onset. The tale of it alters the night.
Intimacy stirs each listener. Each knows the ache.

Entangling glance. Failed
forgetfulness of subsequent weeks, & the shock:
her phone number, his desk. She drops by, he's not there.

But later: she turns up at the party...
Each knows the ache, though only once, & now: the
telling: the subtle eyes, hair. The daring. The first kiss.

As a glance mirrors
anguish & rapture but remains itself.
As a face reveals its lineage but remains itself.

A noise wakes you.
You've been dreaming of figures
you can't remember ever dreaming of.

For a long time you've
seen what they've endured in their lives
& you're grateful to have fresh images of them.

In the night's
silence you feel humbled by
some barely perceptible shift.

Things that were are now
drenched stones drawn back into the sea
& things that will be send word:

the deepest green in a green field.
Rain beats the shed's metal roof at midnight.
You were awake but did not answer

your mind on old matters.
Haven't you waited for this richness?
Haven't you starved & atoned without even knowing it?

Haven't you improvised
to no other end than to witness
these inconstant oracles?

It's in ignorance
we take hold of the actual,
the sky in streaks, in tremors of blue & gray.

Once, immense misery ruled.
Reason & Radiance in a bitter mix.
But ascending, now, from the saddest gasp

passion's twin,
anonymous & indestructible.
So you intuit over ancient words

who once looked down at yourself
from high above as due to an excess of solitude
you could not anticipate

the contour of the banal words
you were embroiled in, there,
in front of a local market.

For years that awkwardness
bothered you. But could it have been
the first of a fullness, the hint of

an intimacy, a whisper of
a rapport beyond mere omen?
However trivial, now,

Wasn't that minor agony,
that unpleasant panic, a death
that had to happen?

Persuasions from galaxies
which flared when the sun was only
scattered threads of energy

blanch the trees, flood the dead man's window,
fall across the volumes of scripture
& pictures of the old world

the book on holy dying & linen still on the bed. Postwar project, the
clock ticking, discolored rug.
An estate, the broker tells you. And that *you*

in what illusion
do you reside, & what
illusion resides in you?

Other images come forward
tentative & then bold: a dancer rises early.
Sunrise, mirror too bright, or does the mirror

decline her gracefulness? Heat's off.
Sweating, difficult. Body turning pure mind.
Only after an hour does she feel among the living.

The fragility that of the poses you read about:
recording session, the singer coaxed by his brother.
Humiliation rising through rigor to effortlessness.

Or a cliff, opening into blank wonder, ghosts there,
great painters bringing color. But there's another report
that's not the transfigured space lovers walk through:

perhaps the elation felt at things seen, heard, felt,
came not from their presence but your transience —
Orange & white: a rivermouth dawn:

each pinnacle of debris cleansed of esteem.
Smoke rising, pier in flame, airplane entering a cloud,
red shell of the sky holding sea & earth.

All are monitions, are mutation, are matter
visible to you in your quickness or are a man & woman.
Each intuits the thought of the other. Each knows:

these echoes are the truer death.
Snow sparkles. Street, never seen with such clarity.
(To become lovers now, even dreaming won't permit it.)

Face, lit. Blond hair, green scarf. The car slows.
(Long ago laws were passed. Now you learn about them.)
The voice not yours: "It's sad to see her dying."

Your restlessness is
the stirring of a woman in sleep
who's pulled the blind, turned her face

into the pillow but the mind
longs for day's radiance & wakes her.
Discomfort chides you, unalert as you are

to the splendor of motion. Your losses,
an uncluttering. The visible invents fresh legends of
anonymity & origin. The bell's recurrent bundle

strikes the brick of day in consonance with a law
both generous & true. Elusiveness fires this plenitude.
(And the visitor so briefly here

what mystery does she embody?) At this hour
what you know of the sun's been sealed into brick
along with straw & the necessity for shelter.

Each rift a continuance — The blue puff
of sky dazzles whoever crosses the dark avenue,
brilliance flooding where the building was.

(Still: you cling to your death.)
As when reading: paragraphs unwinding toward some end
the clarification of old mysteries propels you into

rapport with the unknown. Though
your weariness brings midnight to the afternoon,
your late intensities bring heat & light to a black hour.

Blossom. Brilliance. Festivity.
"Three daughters of the strongest god"
breathe their blessing & conceal an enigma:

that promise you're helpless
to acknowledge casting the light in which you
stand: that it's by the unknown that you shall be known.

Fear alters the course of your secret thought
& night changes, opening into bitterness
& this in turn offers

intimations which
you pursue, shadow, corridor,
labyrinth of what's gone.

———————

For many years you thought
identity your theme, rather than the soul:
appearing first as a woman who doesn't feel well.

Her pain increases, & her fear of doctors,
& the inability of friends to comfort, & the slow eroding
of explanations, & of faith in the act of explanation.

Her words unfold.
She feels her body drawn back.
The unseen claims her, part by part.

Namelessness craves you.
Its purity makes spacious your narrow cell.
It lends a gilt edge to the window's steel mesh.

On the sonogram screen
someone assembles: first:
a trembling at the perimeter of

living darkness, then
thought's bone cup into which
forgetfulness cascades

then the delicately etched organs
like the tracing of a leaf or of coral.
The noble effort's begun & now

the genitals define themselves & take a place
in a series of clarifications as the unknown takes up
the description of itself.

Events plunge into
a radiant tributary & this
deluge cleanses the visible world.

Does this surprise you?
That a theme which seemed so near to you
occurs now as an afterthought,

as trivial incidents become as vivid as
murals in the torchlit chambers of the afterlife
where the soul is first punished

& then rewarded
with fresh uncertainty
exulting in its trial

like a man climbing stairs into
brightness & clarity after a night of
extreme bitterness

& a voice both his own & not
speaks in tones of chastening triumph:
"A hidden grief made me."

Dream: you meet a salesman.
Papers, clothes, knickknacks are gone.
All that's left are body parts.

He opens a metallic case
on the well-tended inner organs
he's refrained from selling until now.

For a while gods were in the world
& then the world was in God & then for a while
both were in words. Now there's nothing but random

gasps & inviolable order. You point the
projector on the lake's surface & this would be
simply to recall the living image of all.

It's night. Your boat
crosses & recrosses the black water
a ghost deep in your thought

& your thought desolate
& irretrievable. Nothing fills the
watery screen. No lord of the lake rises.

Your words are no more than
blood shaken against an altar stone
or the ruffled feathers of a turtledove.

You are meant to read more deeply
in the texts of expiation: *You have lit an alien fire.*
You are cut off from your kin.

Sudden dark. Greygreen tumult.
Sea waves tower. A figure: visible there.
Ghost, your death never was.

An era of lament, all error.
So I read in sleep's dazzle…
A year's gone. I've written nothing:

Orestes, boat sliding back to sea.
Far shore, pyramids loom.
Austere, deathly translations

Seem to be ongoing. Each choice
plots the legend some god's
dreaming. Churning sea.

Wake folding into
a single act. Black dome,
red streak.

Sun a torchlit crossroad,
& the cry: "Cleanse me of the evil
I bear from before the beginning of the world."

Yellow leaves in blue quadrants
where the sky never stops unfurling.
It's not that cruelties no

longer abide but that they are
one variable in a field of white
inscriptions, of futile

& beautiful gestures, some of
which are randomly erased.
The losing cause gains in intensity,

flares out, plunges into the sun.
The mood shifts & shifts again.
A woman begins to speak.

She folds some wax paper & tells of
her father's interment & exile & wandering.
It seems to you as historical inquiry

sweeps continents & cosmologies
into restless water a shelter builds within
the wreckage of intention.

Shadows of the parking garage adrift
on the river. The image of a temple wavering
at the edge of a desert. Caedmon left

unable to sing & a voice said
sing of created beings.
You've waited so long to tell

the story the waiting's become
a major part of what unfolds.
Waking thought more extraordinary

than any dream, — pale blue, the river.
Mirrored tower deflecting fiery
shafts into the water.

No boats now. Gold light wavering.
Silence. Sky's red arc. A momentary
rest in a godly adventure & you

in your isolation are a harbormaster
charting tide & embarkation
& sunlit cloud pattern —

the squares of burning gold.
The interweaving tints of green & white.
The words, edging in & out.

By stillness you
more truly travel who have
too long wandered from death to death.

Through a gate you fly into fire.
The air dipped in blue turns white as the sun rises.
Invisible properties take precedence over

the residue of last night's news —
a darkness the day uncrowns. You're not quite
comfortable with the return of light to the world.

Decisions are made. The wheel of curses
starts turning, & yes, the body takes each breath
but there are times breath itself chooses to revive us,

just as the words earth, fire, ocean, lightning
change the speaker who chooses them
& in their recitation he feels himself become

the listener & the words
are ships crossing a violet ocean.
The storm looms black behind them.

———————————

Brilliance of sail mirroring the sun falling behind you.
How long have you been asleep on this hot, white sand?
You can't say if you're a character in an

unwritten novel, a minor god in a lost hymn,
or whether it's millennia ago under the black & purple
regions of sky. Fleet, billow. Mind's endless ocean.

What rock, euphoric, bleak, & toward which boats race,
cradles you? Not now a figure or shadow of a figure.
Foamtatter. Sunglint. What coast? What horizontal wind?

Each hull, a letter. The fleet, a name.
Bright delirium, mist. Empty mile & oracular tide.
The sky's tremulous enough to suggest terror.

———————————

Nothing can remain in darkness.
All things flicker in the passage of a soul through fire.
An identity has been retracted, an unlikely Helen

whose shawl wove the fiercest volleys
into song. A mother moving among the shades,
no longer adrift on the river of the visible,

& the two cats who meet her,
Chivas & Regal, by some
mysterious grace

have kept their names in the afterlife.
Though invisibility withdraws her body
I remember how her chin

always tilted an inch too high
in keeping with both her piety
& her impertinence

the ghost of whose daughter
brought with a kiss the first of these words
& the consequent shiver gives the poem its form

as over the stony slope
& to the brink of wetness, the
ocean drinks the stone.

Then inkblue, coalblue, grayblue…
ribbons of red behind the island & water
torn from the sky. Glimmer of foam.

Whiteness adding its extreme.
Spectral aperture, land & water distinct,
green stirring in the outline of waves

& surf voicing an interplay of
elements & after what seems like
the longest of nights

yellow & blue build behind
the earth's curve & are
visibility's herald.

The restless cycle of color
has composed a single dawn.
Drenched in death's ebb: day arrives.

Deep within the horizon a star arcs its fire
& flesh finds its own radiance
painful & cries out.

———————————

Your enslaved double's
locked to an oar & lifting the
dead king as the sun plunges into

battle with the dragon of night.
Your calendar's endured such revision
as the wheat's gold cusp & the flood of less

apparent grains rising now in
uncorrelated moisture. You elaborate
yourself from what you yourself began.

You're proved by what forbids you: eyelid's
astonished flutter, — snowflake in spring sun.
Windblown elaborations of an ancient unrest

fire the horizon's crest.
Elation of day's embrace waking you.
The mind's orders appear to be shifting:

In an undiscovered poem by a dead master
you stand at the rail of a boat basin. River, fluent talk.
Boat pulling into inky motion. The sky reddening

& you are outside sleep once again.
As if the purity of speech could also be a vessel.
Or departure & arrival the turning of a single current.

Or you enter at last the world
of the second day. Gold inscription.
Flickering bow: Splendor.

How many versions
of this moment went awry,
botched, scrapped, deleted by

some primal hand
before our translucent
locale turned animate,

and song touched our lips?
Rapid wingbeat: inquiry
lifts into the cosmos

far from the time each blow
was a god with stone altars
& hateful obligations.

Pale ripple of snow,
neither remnant of an old
Creation nor herald of a next.

Icy jag, grey for days.
White fire: heat builds in the
brightening sky. Each context

opening outward so that
even in hell the ecstasy
of doomed lovers

repudiates the flame.
Elsewhere the sun god takes
a human heart in hand & offers

in turn his, the
acolyte's gold shimmer,
the god's body, half gone,

erased by the
elements, as if to defer
to our dissolving witness,

that we're not too pained
by the bliss of their exchange.
Each letter's adorned.

Writhe of vine,
cosmologies carved into
a single verb.

You are lured from
bitterness into the dance.
Your hope has not betrayed you.

Opiate Phobia

At times the real
seems no more than events passing

My clothes are clean
I'm dirty

& these feelings of defilement
are not at all what was requested

verifying
citizenship here

among the esoterica stalls,
among the tears of the treacherous.

Though you are not
the earthly things you see

but soul
& intellect

exceeding the circuit of heaven
your words are drowning audibly now in a red

& irradiated
throat.

All's icing over
& the dream's recurrent

figures
fly away

The Wild Colonial Boy

for Stephen-Paul Martin

A headlong pitch
shattering the whiskey rack.
A pistol smoking in Jackie O's hand...
Dallas did not happen! The
motorcade & magic bullet were a lie!
(Kennedy died in a liquor store in New York City.)
Festival of blood & broken bottles & a last gasp: *Find Bobby*!
The white flame shoots up: & inside the blaze
the driver moves untroubled & slow
& the cab turns to ash
& his wife watches a tape
& his daughter's on the phone.
Knight of Infinite Resignation,
bedridden & devious &
dying untransgressed by the lithium...
Or: naked before a face taped on a mirror
ecstatic & trembling: jagged hair checked by a flower
as stunning as her words are sad:
their crumpled pavilion
a green silk pallor freshened by an interior gasp —
Or: one thought, over & over. Or mania's
desolate glimmer as threadless
through a shattered maze *O
Irish rat berhymned...*
Riot room, a whiff of tear gas.
The time has come. Turn off the tape
& talk candidly with the Strangler
& only one of many survives the plunge
& he remembers nothing of the plane
& nurses or flight attendants
at the airport medical tent murmur
they're often like that at first...
& our biographies are

ocean-soaked clothes & mourners
drift wailing from one heap to the next.
The comedian, flayed. New music
pours from the mouth of a horse.
A whacked dithyramb. Awaited eons,
in darkness. Erzule, goddess & filmmaker,
would lead you through the cool shadowy leaves
to a jungle apocatastasis
but you wander off the path
& into wild bursts of heat & light…
& when the surge falls back
angelic cages & hotel parrots,
fresh juice, mood pills, & in the distance
the blue puff of plastic-wrapped banana trees…
Alright, alright. This time you
be the Consul, & I'll be Yvonne…
Night. Doleful drumming. Negligé & veil.
Demons swirling in the marriage cup.
Soul cut free of the body
& other crude cinematic tricks.
Pilfered crypt, zombie backdrop —
A man in blackface points to
the interior & the sugar harvest
uninterrupted by night. The high breaks.
Nothing helps. Daylong rainy dark.
Deposed in the blue sphere of
my circumnavigations
& Traherne hymns seraphic
from his era of sweetness & terror…
Earth & air, fire & water
A cyclical & ill desire…
World well broken. Shack on a reef.
Nothing's left of that first astonishment
but the candid notations of
a great man's navigator.
Step from the boats, gods of caste, tenancy, bacterial rapture…
Beneath all the upheaval it was an image of herself

within herself & hidden from herself...
& then you flare all
sexiness & wit, a dazzle
in this palace of lobby art
& desktop calendars...
A day with Lulu at the beach...
But you should know, you say,
I am also elsewhere, now, & drowning,
& sending dreams to you across what distance...
On TV: a man with cameras
implanted in his eyes. He blinks.
A screen goes blank. He takes yellow pills.
He never sleeps. He must convince
a dying woman to allow
a film crew at her deathbed...
& the sun ripped from the poster
& all goes spray paint, our drained embrace
in fluorescent zombie light,
our kisses a wrecked cassette tape
shimmering in the trees & burning oleanders.
Toxic Florida. Smoke. Green muck.
How many weapons named after
people can you name? Colt. Bowie.
Guillotine? Not really a weapon.
Lance, after Lancelot. Crossbow,
after Clara Bow. Gatling,
Derringer, Stamp, Big Bertha...
In each moment, a utopian tatter...
I won't drop hints, but I won't
look away. My words are harmless,
you can forget them. But later
you'll be burning, reckless
with intimation. A pure start?
What god could promise it?
Cell by cell intention builds a body,
as arc to a blinding scroll, at the hour
the rabbi unseals it & lifts to

the world the translation of a world.
He moves among the remnant
lofting delicately that which without ritual
would be a defilement to look upon
& all desire themselves unraveled
& read & gathered into an intelligence,
or so I thought in warm rain at the locked gate,
that first temple in the New World…
Or let rivers unblock. Or let green
land rise. Or torment beat you
untillered & towards no home
as angels in gold fire
dispose of messages…

The Reverend Shannon
has retired from Blake's Tours.
He sits with Ava Gardner
overlooking the sea.
The lesbian Baptist voice teacher
from hell has left. The Mexicans
are bare-chested, & dance in the cabana.
He no longer feels the need to kneel
beside sleeping ingénue outcasts.
The Protestant muse has left
some poppy seed tea. Of the cross
& the tour bus distributor cap,
those emblems of divine
& earthly power,
he has, through what,
with some irony, was called
a voluptuous crucifixion,
divested himself…

The Age of Oracles

homage to Nathanael West

I

Twelve phone lines, twelve tapes, twelve horoscopes. A hundred thousand calls a day, a company called *Dial the Stars*. At the heart of each one-minute forecast: a five second plea. A voice within a voice, calling back to the caller: *Write to me. Tell me how the stars have touched your life.*

II

A man files the letters. Grateful, the yellow bin. Merely thankful, the green bin. Hate mail and threats, the black bin. Windowless storage room. Fluorescent glare. A vast wall of market research, to be sorted, labeled, and sent to a further depository. The letters an informal guide to invisible forces: advertising, word-of-mouth, name recognition, and to the operations of the spirit. From every state in the union, messages stream. Countless cries come to rest. Inside each bin, a special box. Exotic postmarks of those bearing witness from far away.

III

A poster on the wall, a drug company promo, a tenant left it when the lease ran out. On it, an alien sunrise, a distant planet, purple deepening into black. What might once have been the earth: now a cold stone rolling into stillness. Behind it, an eruption of red. A fiery flower, out of Dante, lofting an empty world. Rose of the hour, a blossoming narcotic. The annunciation, a list of chemicals. The narrative of salvation, a description of how the chemicals combine, and deaden the nerves, and block out the waves of pain.

IV

There was one last bin, aqua-colored. Disease, despair and death goaded these respondents, lashed them, reducing them to purest need. Beggars at the gate of the invisible, they quoted scripture, told of secret trials and the dreams harrowing their sleep. They implored the astrologer to intercede. Some of the petitioners felt persecuted, some felt suicidally withdrawn from the world. Or sent medical records, or snapshots of the dead. One picture stood out. Funereal crèche, a tiny white coffin. Figures in grief arrayed around it.

V

The mail a continuous chant of voices calling. Long hours, weighing the words, filling the bins. Slowly another world reveals itself to you. A hidden order comes to light. Oracular closet, demographic altar. Who could ever tell the truth of such a place? How the bins resembled a prayer wall, how the slips of paper are one vast petition. How each grievance, complaint, ordeal or coincidence seems, as the weeks and months go by, a page in a book of contemporary martyrs, a book that will never be published. Only Nathanael West. Late hour. Office population dwindling. The coffee machine turned off, the receptionist leaving. In the welling isolation you can feel it, emissary of what afterlife, the burning shade of Nathanael West, standing beside you in the gloom.

VI

When Skylab passed overhead on its final orbit, anxiety touched all who lived in, worked in, or passed through the city. Call volumes shot up. The phone lines went out. A less than apocalyptic hour, but a rage for portents. No one could say where the fiery metal would strike. The hints in the paper were gruesome. The least concerned traveler or resident could not elude an apprehension: deep in the heavens, racing towards him, or towards her, a tiny scrap of annihilation. At such a time, it was hard to accept what thinkers had long argued. It seemed clear: the age of oracles was not over.

VII

Summer, 1980. The evening news: astrology. The murder toll rising in Atlanta. A tangled riverbank, a body, or a part of a body. For a diversion, perhaps from utter desperation, the police allow a psychic to help with the hunt. And so there are reports of mental flashes: the face of the killer coming clear. Photos of the psychic holding bits of cloth or touching the toys of the murdered children.

VIII

After hours. A far-off call. The Southwest, maybe. No one else here. Calm, polite, the caller needs to reach the astrologer. A month ago, he says, his daughter disappeared, walking home from school. Police have given up. A small girl on a dirt road. No clues.

Spectral Evidence

I

Crest,
fiery jag.

Sweep day's shadow.
Turn toward us. Scatter the smoke.

Hidden light, star, stone
brilliant collision

unwritten
gap

Meaning
read in the

rupture of worlds,
Meteor. Fire storm.

Scratch of galactic light.
Pulse of dust in the nothingness.

Break apart our dark —
The blank sky's

folding
back —

II

I see
ritual in ruin

& the deletions of noon.
I see an ocean trembling

& purple welling into the storm's black.
I see a flooded court

& a piano there.
I see

the dream's drowned chord
& the tomb of a vanished acoustical order.

I see
an old book —

spells, trances, chants
bound there in green & gold.

I see a mesmerist who claps twice
& a feverish girl unconscious in her bed.

I see
astral bodies

falling lost through the moonlight
flooding a dead & empty patriarchal eye.

I see
an initial or

initiatory affliction
& the trace of a touch

on the arm or on the back
& broken veins & extracted marrow.

I see
an adept borne

through a series of fears.
A fountain, there. And water

that does not heal —
its white rebounding

falling
blueness.

III

Prophetic hill
Sunken planet

The interpreters gather.
(The hopeless in procession.)

Ongoing hillside offertory fire.
Angel of smoke, all's written out:

dead, dying, unborn.
Petitions. Tokens.

Our earthly names
flicker in the oracular chaff.

Conflagration spills from a holy bowl.
This final dirt's a second Creation —

smudges of nothing
from what was life.

Place of Manifestation.
Place of Dictation.

The pious cry out.
The slain in spirit wither.

The holy mouths are streaming.
The delusional children are chattering…

retelling legends
of holy union.

Sky, ripple & fold.
Daystar terror, dip & err.

The priest crosses the blank womb.
In the char of snapshot, hairlock, letter, thread,

let the pilgrim read the
glory toward which the dead rise.

O *Mater materia,*
Virgin in your fiery circle…

Flare, & foretell.
Spell, from vapor & ash,

The miraculous destruction.
The death of the limits of the visible.

IV

How gently the
bodies are lifted…

the living circling the dead
(the dream's dead ring the sleeper)

no vulture god
no hyena god

no ancestral guide
at the fringe of a fatal place.

Flowing blood & flowing fire.
Diversionary routes. Roadside flare.

But some ghost
of the soul

still hovers, gapes beside the
unscarred & maimed, the curious & dead.

Two worlds touch.
Glass bits. Chrome bits.

So galactic
a scattering —

V

Waking world, a fiery
blue crematory door,

its transom edged with
snapshots & cameos…

Words, names —
aberrations in stone.

(No breeze lifted them.
Death's radiance failed them.)

Cloud shadows flowing
Horizon of sky & sea

As if the mind could hold
only images of other images.

As if the seen & said
raised monuments there

to a life not known
to have occurred.

VI

Absence
of a god's word.

Shades pulled all day.
Undrugged eras before analysis.

With husband, with small son
(who remembers nothing)

Not her sense of exile in a new place.
Not legends & tracts (stigmatae, *docta ignota*.)

Not the cresting of terrors.
The empty church. The voice, there.

The joy of world's
end foretold.

Not those words to her.
Not her words to me, —

Her parables of
a life in time:

a childless widow's
wedding to Christ.

VII

I see
drawn blood

& a drawing close
of shapes the blood calls…

I see waiting, & the
abiding of lives within it

I see
the holy circle

the first & final river
& the rack of blood vials

a medical team divides & adds.
I see a work crew there

removing the walls.
I see jag of panel.

Circuitry unstrung.
Plaster falling in white puffs.

Renovations, a lag in the blood work.
I see no certainties that disturb

no doubts that bring peace
only unbroken delay

I see
opacities in old data

& idiopathic
wavering.

I see a biolab,
a woman, there.

I see the street, a man,
a child with him. I see infant

skin a touch too
readily bruises.

I see blood of their blood,
unbroken yet into

knowable bits. I hear a tune
the two compose in

ignorance & distraction.
I see first light

& galleries lit and locked.
I see pictures on display:

pearl shading into gold.
Mountains, opal waters, shadows.

Ritual figures. Acts of
leisure & of harvest.

Worlds redeemed from green.
I see a seasonal coherence

done in a period style.
Diaspora of color.

Hidden forms:
branch, stone.

VIII

Such light as
places can have —

an X-ray chart held up:
fate read in a rising elevator

(hands of
an intern)

Hospital solarium
barge light & river's black.

Families lay siege here
in vigils binding day to night.

Food, breath & rest are one —
each an attribute of ignorance.

Unearthly ward,
washed-out flesh tones.

Canvas laundry bin
on steel rollers

heaped high
& ungathered

(slowdown
strike's herald)

Fluorescent planetary glow
of the children's wing.

Awaiting evidence
of blood's intent…

Drug allotment.
Oracular clipboard.

Those touched by recovery,
& those touched by its absence…

(Corridors: the lost.
The yet-to-be.)

Dawn, an on-ramp vista.
Brooklyn, a white puff.

No fiery stripe
No blinding water

No *face*
at *floodtide*…

IX

What truth
of origin

What truth of
the origin of lies

What immanence
lost in blowing smoke

What oracular tatter
or rotting scrap

What sentiment in
the sequence of numbers

What discernment in the muck
or clarity in the passing jabber

What epic shadow
falling from the mountain

What puff of dust or
glint from broken letters

What allegory
What corpse

What will be spilled
What chopped up & burned

What gutted or kissed or washed
or ground to powder, or smeared, or eaten

encased in gold
or buried far from the gates

What noise in the brush
What trembling substitution

What terror of
holy calling

sacrificial gasp
or Pentecostal char

What harrowing of
image & word

What building light or
shapes on a far wall fading

What iridescent stone
preceding all color

What sunrise
dead burning star —

What
cry

X

Hot, crowded street
I see a wasp

dying in a bottle
sunlit fury

glitter —
garbage —

A cosmos sucked dry
defiled, bunged in crud

No angel
No insight

No intoxicant
No air

only the error
of having been sent

the knowledge of
the error of that descent

the vivid
wings

Flash Cards

shadows

  Water beating stone. Onrush of want. Each to the other: island, river. Splay, tangle, drop, sob, suck, gasp. Desire touches each. Binds each. Unwinds each. Floods talk, fires quiet. Break, Ache, Heal, Hurt, invisibilities shadow the bed's white.

concrete

  All's a rush job, labor the elixir. Metal made ready, grid in place, the wires bound. Heat, water, crushed core of earth. Fluent onrush, wet stone. What soon will loft: raw flood of grit. Till fiery beds cool and forms rise up: condo, garage, airport, prison.

bar

  Bottles, backlit. Bar mirror, galactic panorama. Liquid fire bound, planetary glass, light out of nowhere. Jubilant glitter, ice mound. Second earth. Bodies flower, flow. Cold video pulse. Day each sip begins. Cortex, spine, chart, from this depth, the meteor's arc.

empty office

  What arrests the erasure, the icy tide, the air, the froth of snow. Not the tower of black glass, the far river. Not the office of the dead man, the executive. Not the last of his effects, the wall photo, the houseboat in Florida, not the portrait of himself, there. Not the salesmen, their hatreds and alliances. Not the new girl, lingering after dark. Not twilight. Not the lover traveling to her. Not the storm.

street

Each dreams of the other. Same night. Same instant of night. In the maze of the other each cries out. The lost cries echo. The echoes are called *daylight*. Corridors. Darkness deepening. For an instant one hears the steps of the wandering other. For an instant the man and woman glimpse each other across a sunlit garden.

domestic interior

A woman, calm now, her forearm, her hand holding it. Bright sink, blood path. Out of that back room, light ebbing there. Couch, the window, the front room calm, opal horizon, flower shop, below. Evening's pink and orange. Gorgeous strata. Watertower, night rising. Ringlet, handcuff, bracelet. The blood's dry. Chemical light. Powder blue, the river, far off, burning sun beyond it, gold, dropping red, a dot. Wine scent in skewed light. Encrusted slash. Nothing's on fire, no pills out.

poster

Volcanic rupture. Red-grained while sand. Light on water in silence. A goat, tethered to a bicycle. Slum huts in green densities. Stone grid in a lagoon basin. Crystals. Thick mud where cattle stray. Ocean nuzzle. Figures asprawl, or entwined, or in thought. Each tiled tomb, a fallen husk. Red lid of sun halved by mountain.

bomb scare

What hot wind. What triumph welling. Empty office tower. Flash of the panic squads. Evacuees mill. Free of the tedium, the meticulous futility, you, also, drift, loose for the afternoon. Monumental looming, black glass, bank, investor. A desert confusion, clarified by fire. Smokeless, as yet. Deathless, as yet. A season flush with drought. Oblivion's runthru: falling jag or endless nothing.

sickbed

You're somewhere else, slowly composing these shadows, thinking out the black spillage of the blanket, the far-off crest of the sheets at your feet, the body, less and less yours, in the distance, quietly devouring itself. The airshaft, cool current, echoes. Above, a radiant fervor, a last puff of color. The shade lifts and settles quietly. Whose dream the days are goes untold.

airshaft

The brightness above varies, but no season really reaches. Rusted staircase. Hollow of stone. Acoustic tomb of voice or broken bottle. Star, planet, brick, page: what high fire dwindling here. Grime-colored luff. Ash-colored flow. The shades drawn, it seems, from the origin of earthly cities until now. Our bodies are shadows within a tower of shadow.

week off work

No pillar, or ordinance, or secret flame. Only invisible vapor rising. Slope and pit. Silence and heat. Blackened stretch of vine. The leaves at last confessing their ashes. Only a drop in the desert, a last cry. And the thought of final things comes like a gift, like a dampness in the night air.

break-in

A gust. An eruption through the rooms. A harrowing has occurred. A rapture of matter. Greased lock, quelled light, empty halls. All's shaken, dumped, ripped, smashed and smeared. A few items grabbed. All else, scattered.

site

Ground barely broken. The bulldozer turns up headstones. Scam or mishap of an earlier age. Identities without bodies. The Hebrew script, the elegant commemoratives. No graves. A search for some record of graves. But the letters have awakened. The names live.

theater

The state wavers. A branch flows, leaves in a girl's arms. Antigone speaks from beyond life. Frail, unbrushed, unwavering, bundled in rough linen, her power one with her hatred of desire. The actress is a friend of yours. You watch, unaware how much you are in love with her. Now she's scattering dirt over the corpse of this world. Now she's exulting in her death. Anger transfigures her. Her words blossom and drift.

celebrities

The hour will come. You will be set free. Voiceless. Bodiless. First flash of last light. Within the unknown, unknowing. Until then, these sales attendants, murderers, legislators, rock stars, doctors, actors, astrologers, generals, gods, models, what you know of them, what you know of yourself, will loom across an illimitable but lesser interiority. Their freedom condemns you. You pause, pass your hands through them. Immaterial figures of a heightened life.

scandal

The case gathers force. Dark facts amass. The testimonials flicker and die out. Once an intimate, now cut loose. And finally, when the knock comes, the papers report, the commissioner, former lord of taxis and parking meters, drives a steak knife through his heart.

news

    Only what's hidden can live. Only secrecy is endless. Word and image, icon and landscape, sound bite and pixel, appear only once. And the told, the whispered, the written, the imagined, the revealed, are also lost, are bodies, are less than bodies, are finally only faces, faces in hell, faces frozen in the ice of a downward path.

birth clinic

    The women here trace ills, debate salves, doctors, sonograms, panic, diet, portent, horrors, talk of pills, things botched, viral incursions, joy, drugs, tremors, love. Some hold fast. Some are at risk. Particulate heartbeat. Thought locking into limbs. Pale eye, gold fire. And the roster, a leather-bound wonder, a black book rife with birth.

gift shop

    The gold pin calls up a pit. Dark, vast. A crater in a rain forest. Occasional gush, flood folding the walls in. Work cite. Grid of string. Staked footage of distant investors. And laborers, hundreds, hacking, hauling, day after day, generation after generation, climbing rope ladders, pulling up the sacks of mud.

homeless

    Across the platform, one apart, closer to the trains. Face up, limbs aligned, like the laid-out victim of an airport massacre. Blankets the color of a greasy garage floor. All who pass are no better than editors, the ones who ordered derelicts corralled, scrubbed, trimmed, shaved, tailored, and posed for a magazine. Morning rush. A cold angel draws close: they are where they are, so that you can be where you are. A chill whisper: they are kept where they are, and you are kept where you are. Urinous wind. Food scraps in shadows. A barn, a zoo, a desecrated temple. And the boots, bright rubber soles poking from under the blanket, are sandals on the feet of Hermes, who traveled galaxies to give you a message, but was stopped.

used books

    Words dead and bound, about the past, about the birth of light in this world, old pages, fold-out star charts, clean and occult, on the sidewalk, on a shred of blanket, hidden words about the sun, where hell is, where, in the beginning, one author says, God placed hell, the blaze of our annunciations, flooding the cool depth of these streets, the high, burning palace, each twist of light the shadow of a soul in torment.

fruit stand

    The harvest blurs, your beauty takes hold. Cool glade in the glare. Wealth of the daylight world. Dark thrall fading. What can these be? Not jewels, not stones. These things you pick up, put down, puzzled, unsatisfied. A few steps from your door, house keys in hand. Creation at your feet. You seem unsure.

Christ Enters Manhattan

> You can't feel right
> Hung in Partiality —
>   —Kerouac, *Mexico City Blues*

I

Air-hammered
risen dust, roadwork.
It's not a banquet.

It's not even
a film of a banquet,
this head of a

garroted
activist moldering
in a dump by the sea.

I have a fire
in my brain how
can you deny me?

The vintner's
daughter dies. Soaked
earth blossoming with deadly

intoxicant.
The fiery tree thins to a puff.
Festival smoke. Does any

ecstatic flicker
light the day's dull
footage?

Grim
imperatives
mix with sunlight.

The writing edges
elsewhere, but also
towards death…

Saying your name, a breathy
vowel in a rapt word, a rapt
world, as in this occult etching

of the brain, the
dark dreamy zones,
the incandescent core…

In the green
asylum of former joy
an intruder blinds me.

Night.
Meteors stream.
Flaring white tremor.

The guide jabs
skyward: "Look. Don't
you see it now?

Those
are what
images are."

II

Meaning needs
denial.
Orison of ra-

diant withdrawal,
tape lifted from the eye,
the one pure organ.

Poster: black —
& a red jag
urging death.

*I felt a snap
inside my head
as I danced...*

Fiery car.
Soul strapped in,
the body's blown clear.

The scream? An
attempt at vision.
Orange welter of sky

flaked with pearl above
a woman astride her lover's mouth.
Or: a suicide note signed: the crucified.

(Centurions
in the ticker tape.
The dog foams.)

This silence will end
& later: the joy, as elsewhere
in this undulant hell —

scraped stone,
rare & mystical leech:
Pharaoh...

Sun's pulse
on scarred rim.
Green prison vista.

Cataclysm,
earth an echo.
(Vanish... cohere...)

Transparent figure
reaching from a hillside.
Fire sweeps the forest isle.

Into what
irradiance
do I erode?

Splayed volume
of a mugged occultist
on a tattered blanket display.

(Help me, holy ancestor
who enrolled in New World
mortuary ledgers the

ever-arriving dead...)
Shadowy blaze,
supernatural flutter

& the waking mind's question —
Am I the body, the coffin, or the mourner
beating his fists against the wood?

Lens open too
long: porch a fury
of white

obliterating light.
(Rapt dismay: your touch.
Which warplane has just stilled

its engine? Which face
hides in the subzero night?
What glitter, what

core, once in-
animate, makes itself
known?

III

What paradise
rises? Headless bird,
bone & ash. Arteries cut:

what feast pulses with that flood?
The powers of the sky are unlocking.
Our quandaries deepen.

Justice, Speech, Death.
Welling clarity, breaking rage,
oblivion flooding the streets…

Evening. Horizon draining of its gold.
Flying snakes die in desert heat.
Babylon fades, in & out.

The rituals of
humiliation regear
& a new scourge rolls.

That corner, a decade back.
A sunlit crowd, a girl struck dead…
Night's a depot: a pipe in a pit

a flare of moonlit sewer
a paper-roofed gully
a dreaming trench

in front of the cathedral…
Primordial pair. Blossom, seed…
Elsewhere clouds enfold our union…

White wall, mapped with shadow.
As you awake scenes of sacrifice flower
scattering you as the one now ash whose blood

still untested
chills in a distant lab.
(Unsettled spirit. I see you.)

Night: so gouged its lunar.
River of stone pouring over wire mesh.
Broken hill, the ditchwork drifting up the street.

Oracle of Egypt, a concrete jag.
Gibberish, a bridge at the burning edge.
What arcadia or morgue…

In seepage of cold. Waiting word:
of glorious thrall, or armies plunging into fire
or how piety, daring, and cruelty rescue the soul from death.

What great change
or annihilation or knowledge
or chaos fresh learning brings to light…

Slain actor, streaked widow.
She speaks with dignity to the camera.
Courthouse steps, the trial a tabloid coda

to the infamous parolee's memoir...
(These began as hers. My cadence betrayed them.
Now they're the murderer's words...)

What destruction
will clear away a world rotting
like the ribs of the boat of the sungod?

Air hammers, dome of the old post office.
Bright architecture, violent hole.
The dream abandons me

leaving less than the prophecy of an exile...
(Within a gently sleeping body
the mind's terrified image

of the body awake
lies shaking, in darkness,
& calling out.)

IV

Angels waver
& Creation fills them...
Sea wind

routes the funeral heat.
Ritual's end: the shovel turns over.
Kin bicker, sad guards at a stone outpost...

It's exile's first day: sky,
watery shred of light's allure.
Invisible fire shaking the dead...

& no longer concealed, one in another,
two within a third, millennial words, unvoiced
& blowing across the earth...

& in parlors, say, in Okinawa,
the message lost in the delicate
carnage of eros…

having shot, twinned, a thin spire
from the shoreleave depth of a drowse
(& the girl looked up, fainted, the novelty of it),

blood & sperm,
(nicked her head on the table
beauty asprawl in her own tide's pool…)

& the sensual man, the sailor, wakes,
trembles, joy's pulse fearful, fallen bride waking,
his twofold gist goes unglossed in the navy's book of love…

Dawn, the fallen
world's red & fiery edge —
terror of that first sunrise

Adam & Eve, reconciled, suicidal.
They consider dashing themselves down in their despair.
Sea's green as astonishing as Eden: light on stone & grass & water…

& what new music
floats through the forest
of a spliced Bible…

Not in this earthly city:
bones & glyphs at the trough
theologies exhumed at a subway site,

death & ecstasy bound in a broken god.
Leveled midtown block, no first dream blows clear:
only graves of slaves, Dutchmen, & British war prisoners…

the body alive
madly distilling the air
& becoming what it craves…

The strikebound & fluorescent
eternities of Intensive Care. Ghostly gowns.
Families loiter. Tattooed & helpless, a father in a black jacket…

So unlit a limbo. Light and shadow mix and unmix.
Bulbs flutter above instruments & bed…
Alert to its limit, the soul jolts…

& the boy, his
preoperative pallor…
worlds verge…

Open,
wounded eye, it's night.
Abrasion one with what's to see.

A material ideality set out in whiplash lines.
Pictorial cup: wave & ripple the mind buries with its dead
as revelation fails, day slows, & things turn to stone. Kick the dirt.

Hours here linked to
those there, head to desk
new to the ritual of the syllable…

I am the tropical bird in the tomb
suspended, in this grouping, above god D
who is none other than the underworld lord, R.

Or the sea beast looming, jaws jammed wide,
gorge within which yet another blows a horn
& holds out a plate offering you

a bone, a hand hewn clean,
& the truest gift a god can give:
a disembodied eye...

Morning paper at midnight,
a minor item moves you: the last of the
Surrealists has died. You feel admonished...

(In the icy pool.
Naked, at night, rings of
my approach break against you

or those of one I coax to further desire you
secret witness to the power of your image mingling in another
with the effect of the knowledge of my watching...)

*But the sip dies
inside me, draws me
into the sun's original fire...*

Attendants hover, minding the tables.
Clients browse. The magazines sorted by gender, age, race,
& preferred violation. Each body in each photo glistens in arcade light

as if touched by that first river, the dew
of the garden quenching these limbs & mysteries —
(at night, a forest. The sky's burning spells euphoria.

The guide speaks:
this will be the poem's last image...
Meteors cutting the jagged ridge of the trees.)

Swiss maids defiled in a wartime field...
Blindfolded or blinded men led by their genitals into a barn
in devotion to the higher regions their acts would mime

& to which we aspire,
through them & in them,
these models with wet parts

prying themselves wide, to where visibility stops,
these sexual martyrs at the cusp of absolute knowledge
as the camera, our host, turns centurion. Booths along the back wall

(Fist Fucking, Black on Black),
ecstatic betrayals & open-mouthed throes
imperfection lost, deep bliss, the body gone...

Leaving New York, two cards turn up.
One from a dead friend, one from one still alive
& on, in fact, a tropical vacation: volcano, black crust.

Ashen sky, the fiery lava seems painted on.
White smoke billows to the card's corner. On the back:
the lost traveler's dream: *Most days up at dawn we eat papayas*

*go to the beach, snorkel, look
at fish, come home, eat some more,
sleep & read & make love...*

And you,
sister, intimate twin,
what clear pool calms you?

Grieving, looking everywhere...
And was that you last night, who set
in my hands a fabulous book

bound in leather & gold —
the high treasure of an
extinct race?

V

In whose thrall will the blade
unpeel the percussive calendar all events hide?
The desert quivers. The light's in bits...

Slowly, a planet floats over the park.
Rhapsodic toy. The tremor of death's unnaming passes through the leaves.
Cosmologies gust, die out. Pure, black sky. The dust dropping back...

Old forces are at war...
There are hostile indications, an
ancestor looming dead at a moonlit desk...

(Scratch mark, acid splash. The visible unfolds.
In the void of metal: a scene.) Crest, fiery face. What stillness will ferry
me to you, who bends close, who whispers, mother lost in wavering
   detail —

Have you lived so
long so quietly
aghast?

Cries of kinship go up.
Red streaks feather a black sky.
Doused torch: sun over crossroads.

Heat in foreign foothills, ruins, blanched,
vacant. Village of the dead. Each family tends its altar...
Glint of gold, adored cameos... The hotel a tomb in the low hills...

Traitors fleece the estate...
A deathbed word undoes a world...
All's gone in a weedy gust...

& face in hands
a demon cut loose from Ulro
flung back through the celestial flow...

the trance of the past replaces your life...
Your curses may or may not work, says the oracle,
but your every gasp lives & dies

a gulp of liquor
stolen a lifetime ago, a trembling
before that first taste that reaches you only now...

Powerlessness, you are lord here.
Graced by you I gouge, scrape, buff & scald.
The copper sheet shows the depth of light receding...

Deepen this wound. Exalt
this agony. Open to me the
abyss within God...

Airshaft, & a brightness.
The brick an almanac of sunlit grime.
Light falls through the windows of the pit...

& far off, ancestral island, drifting,
& this the hour, a hollow carved with pictures,
expressions of an expunged culture, fills with radiance...

That our prayers, chants & names
might be the fading oscillation of a single note
& the labyrinth of the grave conclude in a festival of rain...

but then a voice turns everything to stone...
& then come truths held only for the duration of a thought...
Though you feel like a blind servant

in fact, you are a king.
Throne a barrel of unburied bones...
The royal barge churning seaward in starlight...

The miracles have grown disquieting.
A woman in a black tank top leads me to a zone
of doubling, a mesa deep in the death of this world

*A wet flick chastens me. A pulse
unmoors me. A touch would
scatter me.*

The couple agreed to meet, sky
going black & purple, tide spilling into the courtyard…
empty house. A piano, there. Chords rise, the storm closes…

The abandoned one hears the sea's own dream of music…
& meanwhile the actors are bewildered, in leather
& gold lamé, rendering love's lines…

Flung cutlery, doused bedfire…
Simple objects broken, it's not noon yet…
What judgment, & what court, is not at all clear

& there was another thing the hero
wanted to say, but indifference overcame him
a black flood in an allegorical painting

sky streaming, a crayola'd stopgap of primary colors,
a turbulent limit, a freedom to not return to the brocade of a scarf
as purified souls plunge back through the gate

& thought's broken seal pours fire…
No one can say where the phone calls go,
precincts where permits for the rally are stamped

& a Chief Justice speaks at a banquet…
Nor can you confirm what comes back in a final sunrise
but your consort the King's daughter will not rest until you are free.

Even if you were blind,
she says, this light could not be kept from you,
the kindled hieroglyphs, the cosmos inside the coffin lid…

& death closing from afar
but you were already long established in that kingdom
pointing at distorted & astonishing images of life…

alone in a room in boarding school
in the first of a series of chemical adventures
& weeping from an unforeseen joy

though later comes fear
& panic, then silence & dread
as future lives ripple in passing…

The city across the water barely visible
through pearl-colored mist seems a bleached out etching of itself
an emblematic scratch, a glyph meant to hide some

ordinance about how you should feel…
a dead culture's stone around a penitent's neck…
But the seed cast by the father

is not from the father, but from the sun itself —
fiery threads of solarity across the crates of
liberation theology on a grimy street.

Black twigs in the river's blinding white.
A chaste mania unrolling half an hour each morning…
where in stillness currents of air mingle the black & dazzling script…

Tumult of induction. Surge, falling back —
words in the onrush of branch, river, rising fire
I lean into & echo. Before the slashing letters

plunge back into shadow,
into the tomb of day… The street's
a drawing meant to illustrate the ghostly

dispersal of shapes
& no wind to billow all things
back into the sun.

VI

As in an old book:
not that warring against the dark —
light does not defile itself

& so builds our world, a toy for evil, out of
white blossom & plastic wheels on playground gravel…
Living gods flee the dead city. Dead gods burn the gates of life…

Images only make the eye see
the welling blackness, & all that is not there…
& the child, looking up from the red clatter of his toys —

It's the fate of all objects as they pierce the structure of memory & vanish
into layers of brightness dreamed of by the cults of the last century…
But the space probe pours back other vistas:

an earth too hot to inhabit…
a poison Venus, a city at night where
exhibition graves arrive, in trucks, in chunks…

My parents were gone. Only next door.
I didn't know that. I hid myself. I thought the
Rapture had happened, and I had been left behind…

Open window,
bright ripple of medical forms on the car seat…
the body folds, the soul holds fast —

& in some other inventory of final events the
suicide awaits the rustle of black & blue shadows where light falls back.
And the rockets are seeds of light scattering over the earth...

and the notebook is open, the hand is writing
(defense minister on TV, scanning the rubble).
Seep through me, bleak oracle:

the delicate red spirals,
the shock of blood where
blood should not be...

Sky, a lakebed in a desert.
Beautiful because the shimmer is illusory.
Beautiful because nothing will gather there again...

Today men came to lop off a fallen branch
children played in the tangle, the sudden jungle, pulling off lash
& sword & scattering at the snap of the chainsaw...

Sun beating on the windshield,
blanching the road, the high turning sign
where a gas station marks the turn to the clinic...

The earth a stone,
the book says, *a broken*
stone in the cold grave of the sky...

& leaves stir in the heat, & fall silent,
& you are lost in even smaller annihilations,
the ones Creation can find no place for —

& the time comes & the first words cease flowing
& whole planets of discourse flare out, & hydrogen clouds & stones
& the cool garden in the floodlit shadows goes blank...

& you, calling for a god
of liberation, & your actions
consecrating some repressive fury…

(Close your mouth, the falsity builds.
Close your eyes, destruction fans more brightly.
Cover your ears, the collusion seems a kind of music…)

Uncut gem,
galactic fire closing fast,
the sky at night is the mind of an evil king…

& the city below: a billow guttering raw volume
& a gently viral wind. (To prevent panic, the burials are secret.)
And below the city, torch light, a Lethe of flowing rot…

In hollows, caves & pits
a battle is over. At the banquet,
a formality: the purification of the living.

You erase from the Book of Victory
the names of those who are put to death
& gloss their final cries…

& elsewhere: torn cloud, shape of an eye.
The pupil, the sun. At the core, black letters burning: *lux fiat*.
Animals crawl from the mud, astonished, & human bodies move…

& a skeleton with an ax
stands beside a tree with writing all
over its trunk & leaves…

VII

Our names dissolve,
& the vibration touches all, & the chill
of what will not be, & the natal shiver of what has died…

& I am a woman lost
in the wall's hollow, that empty temple, turning back
the bed a garden in a desert where vines are rats in the lunar rubble...

A clipped ringing,
the other sleeps, a cupped call, voice dropping:
I'm glad I had the child, but I wish I had had it with you...

(A knock. No one's home. No, you're home.
Though now you hear whispering, the back room goes dark.
The police at the door say: someone has called in a suicide here.)

Erosion slowing, the retina
rooting again in the earth of the eye,
but my sight gets worse & worse...

I want to free fire,
the movie maker said,
from our vision of it...

Sky flowing, past lives scatter.
Adrift, pale Esau, deep in a cloud of weeds, & others,
half devoured, like the moon, like the tailfin of a deep dwelling fish...

red & gold, rinse of a chemical river...
& last words: there is no otherness that does not point to unity...
& this could be the crucifixion, or a movie about the crucifixion...

& after the X-ray, the usual walk down the corridor...
& elsewhere day ushers the bride of light into the shrine of the forest &
the long bank line, the exhausted hospital workers talk quietly

& whatever partner you
were, astonished innocent,
preparing for what wedding night...

All's empty, all's a holiday office, phone tape flashing.
A phrase or two as our lives burn: *tear me to bits*. Or: *I'm tired of
dying in this silence*. Or: *Even after, there's a part left begging…*

& the nights are hours in a final afternoon —
& rising from the litter of lost remarks:
a millennial cry…

All's votive bones & wet smoke…
& the steam shovel, ancient grave open,
work stopping, the building, now, may never be…

Plume of sun, horizon, fiery house,
fiery horse, dragging jags of flame through the fields of the sky…
& Zukofsky, seeing above this island the mists of Egypt…

Exile, the meaning of it, deepens. Spire & vault, gargoyle of the wrong god
& bent cells jamming the veins, & it will be another winter of
children with feet too swollen to cross a room…

*hematological memory, that's
what my interest is now, how blood
can hold for years the memory of a virus…*

or as a father might hold a sleeping son to his heart…
& a student named Babak: I lived through the Theater of Cruelty,
the Tehran run. Our friends were hung from what you call cherry pickers…

& Hamid, pale from the fast, prayer rug on the TV…
Empty altar, the mind, pictures loom, rot into words, words
spoken by a voice, a voice which says only: *look at the pictures…*

pictures trembling, a final silence, a flash…
a puff of nothing, a ghost in the grit. Only a graph, soiled & frayed.
Only the Abode of the Holy Ones, tacked on a wall —

& Aramaic, Hebrew & Persian
where we are written out as martyrs
who await the transfiguration of the earth...

Saw my father. He asked so I told him
the upkeep's been tough on the rental properties since he died
& he: they don't let me see anything there, from here...

Phone van at midnight,
air hammers, a door of light in the air.
The pit misdug, the Christ aches elsewhere...

(Belly & bowel, the poison fish
cuts through you, a channel it hangs in,
taking its time, convulsing you with a flick of a fin...)

Invisible star, destroying all carbon...
then came foreign architects with no conception of logos...
No descent, no faces of saints, no gold beam piercing the wall...

Only radiance, welling here as shadow.
Only darkness, within light. Only, flung through space,
this wave of stones the color of an exploded cathedral...

When news of the bad effects broke
I was already elsewhere, pilled out & pure
& floating in the deep blue circuit of air & water...

& each night, news of the day.
Attack cites, television grid. Awaiting
a pattern to our death, & the bright dots flare...

Incidental Eclipse

Pelicans descend
& settle onto Nightmare Bay.
In one life, the shops are closed.
In another, a cataclysm, a harvest festival
where your kisses are a netful of moons and stars
made from foil. But the tremor in the air

The brochure promised our god
would be the one of the second birth,
not just a fox near midnight on the garden wall.
Or a surge of white ocean fog blotting light and sound.
Or words done in party-colored chalk, washed back to stone,
and the summerhouse a char, raked over and sold.
Room of the suicide, a blue cube of sky…
Or a monastery window, constellations glittering.
A drugstore: slip in hand, waiting for a name to be called,
The colors of my aura are dangerously sharpening…
Of the four forbidden subjects, this is the third:
Creation's essential dissolve…

You keep your head half turned away.
On your medallion a glittering river turns into a cloud.
New country where neither the boy nor the girl had ever been.
A bitter mist over a pure lake, lush hairfall, full lips,
there on that hillside, cities scattering out
shrines and pathways though several
from those years are dead
and the sky-high hotel lounge
turning slowly in the clear night air —
stars, the studs and rivets of some further adornment
This is only the first clue to your place here,
your voice cuts in. *The truth all at once*
would only unhinge you…

And they fade, those earlier
bodies, those lucid humiliations —
field where I once stretched out to dry.
Delight, your handmaiden, piercing me…
And the buildings turn to jags and shadows.
Dynamos pulse. Drones fade into the light.
The martyrs are swallowed by their newsreels.
As the sky emulates the ditch: a flowing —
radiance of stone in the deepening mire…
I'm here memorizing a child's face.
The meter on the box goes wild.
She tells me our bodies are eroding.
The pinwheel creaks. The hedge is desolate.
A tinge of blue cannot conceal the sky's whiteness.
Propped in dust, the cardboard ghost house.
A smokeless zone hides in the flames.
In the candle's hypodermic flush
the actress reappears as Memory.
And the clinic is gray, the clients are gray.

And the ditch fills suddenly with poisoned water.
And voices in the empty field will circle there forever…
In one life, a soft calling in the luminous chlorine.
In another, Love's coastal dungeon. Medieval sluice.
I'm going quietly skeletal as infatuation dies out.
Scraps flushed clear, the tide rising.
In the heaven of my last incarnation there will be
wisdom texts on one side of the warehouse
and cheap pornography on the other
and rising from his high bench
the guard will whisper:
Think only of the ecstasy of
the ink flowing from the pen as you
copy out an alphabet you've never seen…

In one sex manual, bodies
are drawn with chiaroscuro and reverence.

In another, breeding takes place atop metal tables...
The curse over the doorway seems to say
that in this quadrant none can know light
apart from what it illumines. Windows,
at most, on a prison isle, their fire
hovering over the water, or mist
clinging in the shadows of a cliff bank
above the bay, the place of the last adepts.
Carved faces: earthly kings on mountain peaks
staring straight up. And below, the invaders in full sail...
And the conversation takes a turn
and out of the blue he's reminiscing
about his hitch in the air force:
There are these heat layers,
radio waves shoot through them
at different speeds and suddenly
far beyond our range a continent
would flash, then disappear.
They call it "ducting"...

Over centuries, fading, surging,
closing you now, a shaped thought
burning, mixing light and dark,
and your feelings prepare an altar
for the knowledge that at last will be yours.
A gift from what distance, brought by what hand...
a communication that says: *The image is a blow*
from a messenger no one can see.
A confusing wound...

The observatory
and the scorched hills concede
a rift between the dead and the living.
And the value of each of us, the stars argue,
results solely from the hidden presence of the others.
And the ditch prays to be raised, and the clouds over the hills.
And the sun's a ghost of the moon

a pale flicker leaves let through the trees.
And the Lord God made the angel of death.
And as a mercy made him ignorant
of what his name means.
In the long moments of shadow,
a molecular trembling from what's ahead.
I hold X-ray paper to my eyes and look up.
The earth's an incidental glimpse.
The past has collapsed,
pulling its light back across the slope.
Trees here don't catch fire, only explode
aiming, as do all finite things,
at endlessness…

Area Elsewhere

Flame at the world's purple rim.
And still: the mole goes on tearing at the roots…
I pluck a snapshot from a branch along the road
wedged in the leaves by one of the departing:
a wedding, a girl in silk, not the bride,
and another, also in silk, they seem to be lost,
wandering a hotel arboretum looking for the feast…
Fields are burning behind the satellite dish.
A helicopter floats above the hospital.
Bitter smoke, blank houses.
A woman turns to a man and says:
in the movie version they will rewrite all this.
They will drop the transcendent order,
the evening glory of sky over the ocean
from which only cold and shadow
have ever reached us…

So Hippolytus, hell's gate:
his wedding speech: he's kissing
some other woman. She tells him a story.
The train they are on shoots past glacial lakes.
Her story keeps changing. She undresses.
The plot becomes difficult to follow.
The train, the talk, and now the sex, race on.
And now the woman has other features and brighter hair
And a tomb of water rises out of the sea…
The holy scroll closes.
The final hour goes unshown…
Dry gold fodder, a hillside of black thistle.
No gate hidden in the radiance
we will wander through in our next trial
prey like never before to the treacheries of rebirth.
Can anyone see the boundary of the garden, one asks.
Can anyone link the bits we've seen, I ask.
What about the trellised path, the circle

in the circle's center? What about
the holy quadrants cut in stone,
the lily pond and the creek?
Not this time. At most:
only a glimpse of matted gold
aflame, and the rippling shadows
that are creatures fleeing…
The child drifts off to sleep,
far from the toy on the night table.
The poisonous remark and the threat,
a white sheen on the grass. The dew
if not the dream has vanished in a heat,
too delicate to be felt as anything but a chill…
You wake up in the office chair of
a friend who has died.
You put his estate in order.
Notepads, pencils, paper clips,
each item studied, ranked by worth.

Darkness pours over the far edge of the city.
When the drawer had been emptied
his life will be complete.
Grief fades. Your attention
slowly turns to judging the one who
year after year saw from this window
what you dream now: tenement alleys
in silver light. Torment? Reward?
This new throne suits you…

Glitter of morning: names ring out.
What rescue lull for those going away?
Breath clouds the color of playground frost.
A photo has come back from deepest space.
The earth is blue and quiet and still,
a silence where curses are nothing.
And the man looks again at the picture
there in a magazine in some waiting room

waiting for word, looking at words:
These royal towers of sky
are only light, light scattered
from dust in orbit around the sun —

Pilgrims and refugees swarm into hills
more of a blackened greenness than these weeds.
Homeland: a police action over the horizon.
Gardens and hotels, a smoking hole.
The fruits of Eden hosed down
a stone gutter. Millennia,
minute, the past flakes away.
The god who dreams our world
does not sleep well. No walls lower.
No gates of jasper. No sudden trench.
Once murdered, he dozes by the sea.
In the sunlit torpor of that uneasy rest
salvation seems no more than bits
of paper scattered at a landfill.
A boat in pieces along the road.
A red circle on the map that marks
the potency of the toxic cloud…

Petals are spilling over a fence.
A mother teaches a boy an old song.
The melody and the words are learned
a half hour a day, first days of summer…
At the piano on the cool portico
they note the pauses in the song.
Mother and son mark and study the gaps
where breath is seized and guarded by the singer.
Rote practice can be exhilarating.
The lungs and throat seem to shimmer.
The oblivion for which this is a rehearsal
remains unknown and distant for each of them.
Finally, there is the matter of pitch.
Imagine, she tells the boy,

an invisible ring floating
above and just beyond the lips.
Imagine no song can be heard
until the words float clear of the mouth
and pass through the ring…

A scattering of boxes
and cartons unfit for hauling.
Bitter fruition, blowing smoke:
a lemon tree at the foot of a stair
beside the soon-to-be-burning houses.
In the Phaedrus, our mortal souls desire
to see again the beauty that has gods in awe
as they cross the sky in glorious rank
and bathe in the radiance of what is.
But some souls can't regain
that world of splendor.
Imperfection pulls us back…
The air is alive with bright grit
or dead with dirty light.

Lost Letter in a Last Word

Kiss me on the mouth,
bridegroom. Rescue me, flame.
Scatter me like a flake of burning shade
through the empty house where a birth occurred.
Make the snowy wedge of the mountain
the first rising of earth from sea.
A woman steps onto the lava flow.
Yellow tent on purple-grained stone.
Pumice-colored sky. Let darkness dissolve
with the last flicker of the first flash…
The one about to be points —
a horizon of ice, asking: *Mother,*
which of our ecstasies will perfect us?
In the glacier, a nook of monastic bones —
the glittering dead who believed,
with Bernard of Clairvaux, true
thought comes as a kiss…

Or a paradisal shimmer
by the crates of cabbages that
almost reach the street. Or gossip
dissolving in a gasp, a whispered name.
Black crease of your jacket, wisp of silver
at your neck, a glint of secrets uttered
once, there, before aspiring to your lips.
Once again we hover in our talk
between lit and unlit regions
in the long black waves of your hair,
you turn away, scan the party, turn back
whispering sad things with such excitement.
Hours break into scattered delight.
Minor joys light the quiet. At dawn
all distance comes to a burning point
our bodies no more than invisible currents
where the light turns gold as ice on a mountain.

Our years might be the final moments of
the unwedded world, you intimate,
when what more truly is
can be inferred from what is not...
And the blue-black shadows slow
in their going, eager to glimpse the beauty
that day hides. And the bride will step out,
a trance fall on the most diffident.
And she will say: *My name is
a letter in a last word...*

As for you, Eros in rotten robes,
amid old magazines. Your career in
fevers long over, how busy you've been.
A decade, now, into your new life as an actor,
as a walk-on in a variety of TV shows.
In the latest, the doors of the set
swing oddly open. The cops enter,
nervous. The room's been "tossed."
Corpse, haggard, in shadows. Whiskey,
powder, money on the table. The TV glowing.
Deathly grizzle in the cartoon light. The
rookie checks your vitals. *Hey Sarge,
this guy's been dead for days...*

Come to me, truth of the sun,
through some opening in my head.
Come to me, in the long lull between
first and last — a glance, a greeting,
a touch, a drowse. Utopian
tremors in a dark room...

A Parish in the North

A girl with the "gift of blood" kneels at
a gathering. The Ghost speaks through her…
Later, in the woods, a schoolboy awakes.
The streams have turned arterial.
The trees are made of flesh.
On Starr Avenue, a holy medal
lies hot to the touch beside the corpse.
On Fairview Street, day drains into low hills…

(Perils are great now, powers are great now.)

If I say surely the darkness

shall cover me, even the night

shall be light about me…

On Mansur Street, the night air's
all voltage. An invisible burning spilling
from limbs to chest. Panic whispers: if this fire
reaches your head, you're dead. While
across the room, the TV preacher
faces the camera and says:
I see a woman who is very upset,
in a chair, in the cold, in an old shawl
from someone who has died…

In Europe, observatories report
a dark light hidden behind distant stars.
Since time began that light was there, they say,
a black radiance reaching earth only now.
Light of the hour, let all be nothing.
Vandals remove the head of the crucified
on the cross on the promontory by the waterfall.
Thieves lift the hands. The once lit

immigrant church goes dark.
No one guards the grounds.
The diocese can't afford repairs.
The roof's a hazard. In the end, marble
is torn from the altar, desanctified and sold.
Wrecking ball, the high dome topples into itself...
I wake up, and someone's there
in the dark. I'm irritated and afraid.
In fact, I'm shaking. And then I know
who and I say: Anne, what do you want?
And she says: I know that I'm dead,
but fear still torments me, mostly
about my kids. Could you please,
please, look after them?

Memorial Auditorium, rented out.
Pentecostal Catholics in a light snow,
their guest a girl, arrive and enter,
touring from Venezuela, telling how
the wounds of Christ opened
the depths of her flesh to the world.
At a lull in the fervor, pleas are written
on scraps of paper, folded, sent forward.
They are petals gathered into baskets which
the girl with the gift of blood accepts.
She pours them into altar bins.
Banners glow in a ring around her.
The names of the sick are read out loud.
Devastations come to mind. (A niece, say,
dead for days, folded up on the bathroom floor.
Her junkie boyfriend out cashing her checks.)
The stigmata lifts a rose into the air
as if from the gash in her side.

Circulars, email, flyers, faxes,
newsletters, videocam Internet files,
— the sun spinning in the sky or dipping down —

quips from children who speak to the Virgin.
Hills of Eastern Europe, whispered about
in the back of churches in Chicago,
by a rack of prayer cards, in online
chatrooms dedicated to the dark time
or in Korea, over discount long distance —
(Perils are great now, powers are great now.)
The ecstasies are erratic. The telling,
continual. *One line only in the blur
of God's book could I really read.
Not even one line, a part of a line.
The part ordering me to sing…*

Hints and symbols die out.
All's actual now. Image & cadence
from archaic accounts can be dropped…
*Let autopsies open the chambers
of our hearts. Let men of science find in
our nerves the likeness of pillar and scourge.*
A boy presses his cheek to a stone bench.
Crows on snow lift into reddening sky.
In Africa and Kansas and Taiwan
the same dreams have been recounted.
These dreams may be the last ever
to settle into an unraptured skull —
*I was standing in front of my old house
by the wheelchair ramp installed for my father.
It was night, helicopters overhead,
gunfire, sound of explosions…*

This was foretold elsewhere.
This is happening here and now…
A pietà on the porch. A trembling
in the night sky, as seen in Venezuela
last week, blue and green around the moon.
And late at night, in an empty church,
a secret adoration. A woman

at the feet of Jesus, His suffering
heart crowned, with briars
visible amid petals of gold fire.
Broken before the unbroken icon,
she requests assistance for her son.
(Some misfortune. Could be medical.)
In less than a whisper, the reply:
To enter my heart, you must
pass through the thorns.

Parade Route
(1993)

I

That fuck is some slow croaker
the nurse quips, rag in hand, & a chrome bowl —
dying days on end, an asshole to the last
Or maybe a Pharaoh, lost in loops of air,
Osirian snag of a ventilator…
Later, at the end of the street,
a store window flashes, all video.
A multiscreen strobe of explosions
striping the lunar night of an icy gutter.
Bodies and smoke. Not the news —
(World Trade in flames!)
but almost the news:
Towering Inferno.
Burn the veil, Imam.
Turn all to the glow that was
before this light was the only light…

Before some other village
truth rolls in along the trade routes.
Metropolitan death cults, leaving no records.
The outrage of disinterested witnesses is our only guide.
Xeroxing here, in the purgatory of part-time jobs,
the failing fire that spares the world…
Tacitus gossips in the gardens of Nero…
Gibbon films the path of Attis through Rome…
I remain, for now, a midtown temp
or a prisoner on an alien planet.
Either way, gravity slows all motion.
The air devours sound. And the distance
from morning to evening seems interstellar…

Tomorrow kicks off a citywide
Disintegration Festival. Racks, displays,
flowers, carts, booths, reviewing stands, rides.
All's spelled out, now, for newcomers and those
whose minds might wander, in gold letters
along the side of the Oblivion Flotilla...
Among the celebrants might be
the legendary depressive, Daphne M,
for whom entering the office each morning
was like walking through a whirlwind of broken glass...

The Redemptive Agony Arcade
hums in the shadow of the cineplex.
Children of the cult sing in the stairwell.
We live in a burned-out detention center
or a Botticelli sketch of Heaven.
(What wisp of us will outlast the light?
What spirit, what tender pencil outline?)
Pierce the pit, gold beam, the maw
of stone and shadow, street and door.
Spill down, remnant radiance,
where the world occurs. Glorify
the bits of truck in the rubble,
the orange nets on the scaffold...

II

Next morning, the banners lie flat.
One says simply: these words are burning.
One says: we are the residue of what will be.
Biscuits and glass bits glitter on the street.
One banner says: *v'tzi-va-nu l'had-lik ner.*
Another says: our blood cells shake
from addictions that have yet to occur.
Along the route, a psychedelic bedsheet
calls out: *Every several gate was of one pearl.*

& a T-shirt, streaked with the dark tones of gutter water
& a vacation poster the color of the blue
plunging abyss of the sky...
Messiah soda. Ezekiel pinwheel...
A last helium balloon scuttles up
through the black cast of a skyscraper.
Renewal has concluded. What god graces
that splatter across the law school stair?
Hidden one, make us witness to your will...
The blossoms in the trees are cups of dust.
Tomorrow, a film crew rigs the park with
body parts. An apocalypse, done with props.
Limbs in green branches, a head under a bench.

Scandalized Masks

In the experimental theater
above the darkened slaughterhouse
the satyrs and Amazons are painted green.
Then Troy's falling. Then all's panic
and historical torch smoke...
Outside, kids watch a car in flames.
Heat spells and dust. Sunlight whitens the air.
(Kokoschka, Strindberg and Kleist are looking on.)
We can have sex if you want, but I've got this infection.
I'm bleeding, I mean all over the place.
My doctor is frantic. My body is
a nightmare I have to live inside of...
The days lag, like a raffle in a parking lot.
(The telescope's askew. The horizon is vertical.)
Balloons fly over a dome. The sky pours purple.
Dark moods sweep across far continents.
An art student writes a manifesto.
Spiritual plagues are forecast.
The bakery called. You left your
credit cards scattered all across the
counter. Bring some ID. (Talk to Patty.)
These routines rage in the mind of
a dead comedian, one found horribly
transgressed in a Nevada motel. The heat
makes for martyrs. Joan of Arc. Her face
moves the foot soldiers, there at the pyre:
vraiment, elle était la femme de Dieu...
& other loves seem less. One to the other:
That thing you told me, that you took pride in?
Well someone else went there after you did
and they did what you did but did it better
than you did and now no one there
remembers anything about you...
Another says to another: *I feel terrible.*
We were having lunch, and suddenly I feel terrible.

Something you said totally depressed me...
— I was talking about something I want to do —
Yes, it was something you wanted to do.
Something you thought you had a chance of doing.
Someone had described a possibility to you
and you had taken that as encouragement...
Another, confiding in silence to another:
Who are you, that I feed all I am
to the flicker of your image in my mind?
Another, whispering in a library, says only:
I once got a postcard from a friend
who took nude pictures of me years ago.
The card showed my body. But guess what?
I didn't even make out me, cropped as I was
at the neck and knees. It's very strange
to see yourself naked, and without a head!
Dignity and outrage convulse the air
in fricatives, dentals, labials, and wailing,
night after night, for the length of the run...
Medea mixed with *The Trojan Women*
& key bits of *Iphigenia at Aulis*.
The parapet is high up and all around.
The air is bad all over Cancer Valley today.
A child wakes screaming from a dream
of a huge yellow spider floating
beneath the surface of a lake.
A spastic wallops a woman on
crutches in the pharmacy doorway.
Children lay flowers on the riverbank
for the murdered girl in the picnic cooler.
And at night you hear what sounds like rain
but the grieving dead do not want to come back.
(Bad air, out-of-service power grids.)
Grace drains out of me. I am angry
and disoriented. I feel like a Christ
who has been surreptitiously touche...
The sweat of day takes hold early.

The cleanup league rakes the chunks,
the flowering mud that hides the subway vent.
You dream you've found the old apartment
you rented one summer with an actress.
The troupe broke up long ago.
The director went back to Russia.
The mythological extravagance
you all worked for was never staged,
that burlesque with a violent end
and buckets of stage blood…

For Edmund Spenser

The aura of the planets
around your skull, and arrows,
twelve, piercing different body parts —
each shaft marks the rule of a starry house.
Paralyzed knight, dipped in sweat,
you can see the cup, but never claim it…
The hypnosis has had some effect.
A part of my brain is awake
& telling me to wake up.
Though I can't stop
I can hear my own voice
yelling at me to stop. The pain
starts between the bones shooting long
threads through the limbs.

The lesson about the vitality
of antique symbols slows a moment,
as the philosopher frees a fresh mouse.
The pet snake strikes. Everyone there
dreams what the mouse feels: fear,
bewilderment, or as the jaws flare: joy.
(Apprehensions of the beautiful prove
more and more distracting, and all
catastrophe seems a gloss
on the ascension of the soul…)
Then in the candlelight, I coughed.
The spasm blew out a joint, the muscle
bit into the nerve. Sciatic sword blow,
I doubled up. Pain shot through
the right leg, I writhed, let out a cry,
and our romantic dinner was over…

Later, at the tattoo parlor,
a scorpion curling above your heart,
the small talk came to rest on the matter

of piercing: what can loop through what.
What hang from, by, beneath.
What cuts and where. The wounds,
the blood, the weight, the sudden gap
where air and light circulate through the body…
Later at a gallery opening, back against a white wall.
She turns her head, Duessa, 20 years back,
the pale translucent skin, the sharp nose,
expression, confident but slightly lost,
or tobacco-sweet, sardonic and dreamy,
smoke in chill predawn blue bedroom air,
her pre-Raphaelite glimmer,
with a notebook full of
beautiful fables and bitter portraits —
a postcard medieval demon over the bed…
In the annals of Arcadia, all this will shine —
though the shrieks & slammed phone, just now,
hint that your salvation has met with delay.

You begin writing the epic of your exile
at dawn, at the office, in wet shoes —
When I lived in Fort Lauderdale
I had inch-long nails. On each one
a pastoral: a desert, a beach, a lobby, a cloud,
the Holy Land, the state capitol, a tomb, a fizzy drink…
O Knight of Intermittent Mania,
in the dungeon of daylight while your
double rides in triumph through the castle gates,
defeat strings your crest on a tree of shields.
A head blow whacks the quest clean out of you.
The monster in the forest will be slain
by some exemplar other than you.
Acrasia sucks out the soul, kissing your eyelids.
Or wandering around in the wandering wood,
your skull crammed with past lives.
With ghosts from far back,
called by the bones and flowing blood

of who you were, thrill of lives coming clear.
Or lustless, at the Pentecost table...
I bruised myself terribly last night.
No one could wake me...

There is no explanation for
how things are. The silence proves only
that you are dumb with pain, on the one hand
maintaining your professional status
and on the other doubled over and
bruised from a beating, devils
out of the air, from afar,
like a figure in a woodcut
from the *Malleus Maleficarum*...
When you've had as much surgery
as I've had, barometric pressure is hell.

The White Tomb
for Edward Foster

A coronal spree. *Symbolisme,*
adrift in America. Adepts of the '90s.
The gifted, never quite mastering a style.
Saltus, Fawcett, McIlvaine, O'Sullivan.
Lords, once brilliant, now ghosts, on the
nod above once habitual loves…
It was as if the mind of the world
were dead, and the time had come
to distribute the souvenirs…
The dreamer arrives for a party.
A strenuous beating has occurred.
The host pulls him aside: whispering,
you're here early, come back next week…
Get Larry to tell you about the death orgasm,
the bride-to-be sang, later, the red moon
an alchemical huppah over Central Park.
Believe me, it will never be confused with sex…
Evening floods the dawn. By noon it's night.
You're in a forest. You're a girl in a white gown
who sweetly dreams within the grave
of a remembered conversation…
I have to get to the Immigration Office.
Does anyone on this train speak French?
And the weather diagram for today —
A small cloud gulped by a restless sun.
At the champagne brunch, a moan
about the limits of eroticism — *I feel*
continually drawn in, but never inside…
that snowdrift of a dream, that Nebraska,
where each of the two dies curled and alone,
cold as a polar wind over a prairie…
A ranter in the train terminal
in Hoboken hails eruptions on the sun,
fiery exfoliation, three times the size of earth.

His question: *Now do you know who God is?* —
fills the vault of the waiting room.
And across the ferry dock, the glittering river,
wings your answer: *One more detail from a distant time
that scholars associate with intense passion.*
Ashes will never be so scattered by wind
as you are by these desolations.
Now, the neurological storm
telling what's coming shoots fire
down the pathways of your left arm…
*They found the ambassador,
my father, wandering in a desert
naked, out of his mind. Social Services
begged him, an American with
wealthy parents. He had a condo
any Israeli would die for, overlooking
Gethsemane and the Wailing Wall.
He destroyed it, top to bottom,
turning everything into art.
He slept on an unhinged door,
his only furniture, an old Mr. Coffee.
He mixed ashes into wax and called it
the face of God. I had just come
from photographing an ossuary
in the mountains of Hungary.
Femurs hung like wind chimes.
The floor was dirt from Golgotha,
hauled, in the 12th century,
at considerable expense.*

Neon in Daylight

Homes empty and burning,
there's beauty in the tracking shot.
After the deportation, lush vacant dells
on a TV show about the recent past.
(Or a junk mail flyer, brightly colored,
about depression: trials and traits
such as useless expertise or
lack of empathy, chronic rage or
failures to integrate changes in mood.)
Meanwhile, the sky spills purple in the east.
What sun falling over what far hills
like a horribly askew space shot
about to burn the dry fields of
the heartland to the root
and all the wilds of elsewhere
that catalogue of Expressionist prints.
That gnostic gossip, that truth at lunch —
You remember Tex? The guy with the luck
to be run over by a judge in a Rolls Royce?
(The judge died during the suit.
Tex got a serious whack at the estate.)
Well, his inner organs probably won't
last a lifetime, but he's bought himself
a horse farm in Oregon…

Intergalactic hole or home
& the stars, a diaspora esplanade
of old chains, burning tires, car batteries.
The clouds are cities torched in foreign wars,
are the scattering of what might yet be
or a world ripped secretly in two.
Hidden in the halves, four new realms.
Touched by your attention, each
illumines another nine: in one or all
you might live, but some enchantment

demands that you abide in a booth. Four
screens. Four porn channels for each screen.
Push a button, see lips on closed eyelids.
The impulsive clutch in the gazebo.
The forgiving or feigning turn —
see more than a moment can hold.
At the end of the block, a repair crew
has gouged a long trench along the gutter.
Boys, girls, faces close, on benches by the park.
Their words would prove words are nothing,
only a hypnotic wavering of the lips.
A shadow sweeps across the street.
Flash after flash now, in the chalky black.
Clouds clear, but when you close your eyes
later in the dark the shudder of light
goes utopic inside your skull.
Shot incarnation: an old menu
taped on a wall. And on the floor?
A swizzle stick: a red plastic monkey.
So much boxed and shipped, the room
looks as if the Nazis swept through,
forgetting only a gift certificate that
dropped behind the radiator.

Here / Beyond

The Eden exhibit's closed today —

all those illustrations for *Paradise Lost*
done by a lunatic at the end of the last century

note the erratic sense of scale…

Sonic bits of what's ahead reach you
as across the spacious interior

a crystalline mansion, or a rubble lot

where cops say, *get out of here*,
(and this your old school playground).

First night here / beyond

Red brick in wreckage dust.
The convent wall still standing.
You're ecstatic. In an instant your
twin will arrive, will get all this…

Pure white mist from a heated pool.

Rectangles, a green inside a white one,
luminous and empty, but for the shallows
where a boy takes a swimming lesson.

Anxious queries, in the low mist, sapphire
glow and a woman, hip-deep, coaxing him.

He's afraid of floating on his back.
Head tilting, arms out, he begins to drift.
He looks up at the pale blue hole in the sky
through which gold, purple and pink are pouring…

The second night, a world tossed
like a bloodied rag on the seat of a bus…

Think of the destruction of the temple,
whispers your guide, *the fruit of that ruin.*

Without that calamity, thought would not exist.

You'd have only pure nothing in your head.

Then she points to the stars visible through
a window in the ceiling of the plane…

The third night dies: a love letter,
a blue blur pinched from a gutter like
a photo lifted from the fluid tray —
*I am looking out at flowers
on an apple tree*, the lost one
writes, to one far-off, *the one left
from when this was an orchard…*

On the fourth night, Enoch,
you unlock the archive-of-what-is.
You read the book mottled with myrrh —

*Blood covers me. The blade,
spousal, keeps working my back,
shoulders & neck. I'm at my task,*

*washing dinner plates. The dream
opens my body to the night air.*

*Warm water rushing from the tap.
In the window over the sink: stars.
Air & light sweeping through me.*

My blood evaporating.
Some vast circulatory joy
completing itself in my veins…

Next night, the angel's jibe
would harry the glitter from the dew
in a field with a dozen gulls & one crow.
Meanwhile, a hint of a whirlwind —
far end of the street where no
prophet was last seen…

Night, a night of sunlight.

Old worlds, new puzzle
from a museum gift shop.
The Aegean glows. Shrines
and empires rise. A lost library.
Then the renaissance stalls.
The mother says to the
children, there on a patch of
sunlit carpet: *We have to*
think, if we can't find a piece
now, we've done something wrong…

Sixth arc of the spirit. A reroute.

Houses dark. Light in a back window.
Neon-ringed signs. Accountant. Masseuse.
Dealers in guns, coins, cards. Alarm glow
in locked shops. South of the airport,
devotees in trailers, dumped by
aliens in a wet hell. Truck parts
on lots, apocalyptic decals,
drums, cylinders, squares of
plywood, rotting in stacks.
These bits stare out
like dumbstruck skulls
on a mortuary totem pole …

The complete is prior to

the incomplete. But in coming

to be, the incomplete is

temporarily prior to the complete…

Aria Nowhere
in memory of my mother

Where are you?
That's what the wind says
as it scatters blossoms over the earth.
The face I long to look upon has disappeared,
that's what the field flowers say
at the cusp of their color.

Without that voice to call me
I am motionless, says the deer
as evening lifts over the mountain.
Where is the one who will sit beside me
in my sickness, says the child in his room.
Who will share this with me, says one
struck sad amid the feasting.
Where are the dry twigs
and scraps of paper, says
the uncreated fire on behalf of
which the match is struck.

Weeds range into the garden.
The poison languishes in the shed,
and the bottles of polish and cleaning fluid.
Chemicals, inert. No catalyst breaks the quiet.
The house is empty, and all the rooms of the house.
Where is the one who will set me in the earth,
says the tomato plant in the paper cup.

And where is the grave we are
bunched and waiting for, say
the flowers on the table.
Where are my mourners,
says the body in the coffin
in the parlor at night.

The water under the dock
in front of a well-lit warehouse
at the other end of the continent
asks, where is the current that
once brought news from far away?
And where is the trumpet of judgment,
say the hills and gullies of the Holy Land.
And the nurse who stood all night
beside the deathbed
feels the heat of the sun
face to the sky, lying on a beach,
on a vacation, a thousand miles away.
And in places around the world the root
seeks nourishment, but the ground
has turned against it.
And the air cries out, beaten
by the wings of birds. Radio bands
have been cleansed of notes and chatter.
There is nothing to hear but the final silence,
reaching ever further below the crust of the earth,
where the tremor cannot find the fault
and passes deeper into the stone.
And the star collapsing at the fringe of time
calls to the last light that will
ever escape it,
you belong inside me,
there will never be a home
for you anywhere else. But the light
ignores the cry of the star and speeds on…

I fly up a mountain
looking for you, says one of
the bewitched children in a dream.
But fog covers the peak, the inlet,
the islands, nothing can be seen today.
All I take away is the cool dampening
of my clothes. And the falling snow

asks where is the mountainside
promised by the clouds.
And the gold sear
on the high white fields
will never achieve its glitter.
Where are the beautiful tresses
and the mischief of the wind that only
I could quell, asks the hairbrush on the table.
A pillow welling with its blue oriental silks
tipped with gold frays, glows in mild sunlight,
asking, where is the grieving face
that will press against my emblems?
And in a variety of fires around the world
burning seems bewildered by the lack of smoke.
The smoke seems confused by the death
of the wind. The wind lies quiet,
unconsoled by the galaxies
glittering beyond it.
I sent the birds to find you,
says the gold tree in a fairy tale.
The unripe plum on a green branch
that cannot choose within itself a color
luscious enough for the season
has heard nothing of you.
The newborn goat grazing
amid the peaceful flock
has seen nothing of you.
The fish at the bottom of the lake
in the shadows under the bright reef
offers no details. Ashes in the jetstream
that rings the planet report no memory of you.
It seems the one I want to speak to
has not been noticed anywhere.
Perhaps the only hope that can exist
is the hope than remains unknown, says
the hot spring bubbling through the night.
And for one hour each night anyone

can still be healed, but no one
knows about it. The halt are asleep.
The lame drift off. The crippled,
hauled from their rack, have been
washed, fed, and sedated.

The dead one appears
but the living have fallen asleep.
The dead one fades, truths unsaid.
Up the street, a hammer strikes a nail,
and in the whole valley, in the whole
regency of midsummer splendor
there is only one sound,
a hammer striking a nail.
How pointless altars are now.
Now the entire earth is a single altar,
say the mountains rising across the water.
The days are shortening.
Ice fills the channels.
The coat of the fox turns white.
The nesting grounds are blown away.
The foragers depart, the sun is defeated.
All's quiet as the ocean floor
where the wreck lies.
And the storm wanders,
asking, where is the land?
And where are the apples,
so many last year, now so few,
the child asks, white smoke trailing
into a stormy sky or a dome
the color of a light-filled sky
and the sky lies broken
into bits above it.

Occult Blood

The clock's a palm-sized skull
with a tiny hinge. Split the dome wide.
Skeleton arms guide the eye to the hour…
Revelers walk through a hurricane
spun down to a tropical storm.
Only last Thursday did I
disintoxicate myself
of a lifelong misperception…
Chlorophyll drips from the leaves.
(I prefer not to say, the year is dying.
Only, the green deceived me.)
In the evening, attention will rest
on the newfound cracks in the chimney
& the escape route of smoke through the sky
that alchemical woodcut of a man
his abdomen peeled back
his entrails, a galactic swirling.
Latitude is little more than a glance at the stars;
but to know where, crossing an ocean
in an old ship, you really are
pitched the TV auction man
with a chronometer,
you need to know the time…
(I prefer not to say the numbers
slip my mind. Only, the calculation
in torrents sweeps away half the coast.)
Occult blood, blood where it should not be.
Like an eerie light in a forest. Like a tape of birdsong
in the tunnel made up like a grotto that leads
to the admission desk of a clinic.
Sunset soaks the altar of the horizon.
(Not, the air trembles with the dread of the lamb.
Only, the air fills with notes from a horn.)
Occult blood, hidden blood.
Forget that far-off tropical retreat

where Hitlerati and proto-environmentalist
Charles Lindbergh, slowly fading,
frets about the gutters
on his tomb. In the end all
will be a party, a sugar skull
on the Day of the Dead…
And a woman by a wall,
in a wild red low-cut dress.
And a man, his tinfoil hat
shaped like a ferryboat.

Life Outside the Gutter Factory
for John Olson

Then the wedding party
turns eerie. At the group portrait
the bride and groom are tight-lipped.
Bunched in a field, everyone wears shades
as if on the horizon behind the camera
a nuclear blast were occurring.
Meanwhile comes the news
the concert is canceled —
Hildegard of Bingen…
whose divine harmonies still
enchant the factory where you paint
gutter drains with bright colors —
a change from your old job,
camouflaging battleships…
For you the rivers are gutters,
the valley becomes a gutter, the streets
are gutters in the flood, fish swim through them.
The slope of the mountain is also a gutter,
and the crevice in the bark of a tree.
The sky forms a gutter of clouds
of light, of air, the body is a gutter
waves of feeling flow through it
as the visible world's a gutter
through which light pours
as through a ring of weeds
as through a chute of icy water
as through a cylinder of stone,
a dreaming depth where you drop
astride a bicycle, one recently manned
headlong and brakeless down a snowy peak.
Overhead, the hole in the ice glows.
But the water is turning black.
No chance now, to count meteors.
But you can feel the sky on your skin.

You feel yourself torn by light…
Airplane parts fall into the swamp.
Control bolts, aerial refueling hoses,
rocket pods, strobes the size of basketballs.
Towns tremble under the flight path.
The storm season has begun.
Over at the embassy party
a woman reaches out
almost cupping your elbow
turns her head slightly away
a light blush rises through her face,
you have no idea what you were saying…
Electricity streamed through me
once, when I was a boy in Mississippi,
then crackled around my brother's head…
Hail in sunlight, black clouds flare.
Rain, throttling full. Lightning wires
detonate the sky. Animals
crawling to their homes…
Hopeless gutters, overrun
in the spill of planetary radiance.
Not clear now, what flows through what.
Abolished channels, wet with what splendor.
The mountains are locked. Roads crack.
Implacable shimmer of sun on water.
Not for nothing, you tell yourself,
that old initiation ritual, your
back skewered with needles…
I want to say one thing, she said,
through the perfume and silk of evening
and actually say endless things…
Driving through Tunisia
with an apparently garbled fax.
A sky map, drawn by hand in Tacoma.
An instruction, that makes no sense.
My husband, half a world away,
how could he have known?

But as the fax foretold
a few inches left of the star
the night sky shot through
with ethereal light.

Targets, Mongolia

after a painting by Randy Hayes

A world dipped in dye, in solar fire, yellow and gold, threaded with orange. On or in that world, an image denying that light. A field in Mongolia. Archery targets on a dry plain, askew, tilted toward the sky.

*

The sky flows pink and orange, over the earth-colored cloud rim and the low, distant hills. Behind the targets, a horizon slab, greenish gray. Then wet streaks and a sullen glow, a sodden hollow, a glint of copper in the terrain. Cloud shadows, closing in or blowing away. One cloud's a ravine of white, a fray of fire.

*

When translucence arrives, all's over. Some unseen arm seems about to sweep the world away. Paintspills, a shawl. The folds are opening. A revelatory gesture. Could be a dancer in India, a prostitute in Milan, a transvestite in Seattle…

*

But the end, here, should be "out there." Take the targets for an ultimate outpost, a sky monitor hidden at the quietest edge of the world. Presume recurrence in the scattering from a quadrant, a Creation whose initial light showers the earth only how. Prove as possible, if only for yourself, what Plotinus said: *A word softly spoken can influence a distant object, and obtain a hearing from what is vastly remote in space.*

*

Cloud, sky, mountain, plain, all dissolve into a monk's bed, a row of gold masks, a wrecked temple. The paint clears. The photos, printed on the canvas, dipped in dye, slowly stand out: an old tomb. Artisans making statues of the Buddha. Men with a monkey on the way to a festival. Camels, motorcycles, interiors of a dilapidated hotel. Atavistic figurines from an overtaken faith. The edge of a roof. A train track or tread. A necklace from the grave of a prince and his consort…

*

The targets are tilted back. The arrows must arc. The archer must be, have been, far. One feels the sun warming his back. Sees a storm steal his aim as he shoots. Sees darkness scattering before him, with one shot…

*

Perhaps this was a training camp for low-tech terrorists. Or trash from a festival. The targets angle away from each other. No solo marksman. But the hint of fellowship darkens the mood. If once there were two, they could only be far apart. Now and then dust would cloud that innermost circle. Each assassin-to-be waits for the wind to drop.

*

Could be the Orphic cults began in this field. Their renunciations, a flood filling the well of Western thought. Could be their devotion persists. Violent one, you saved the Trojans for a while, then destroyed them. Arrows of your light are falling through the clouds.

*

Or beams from lost galaxies. Or scraps of the first flash. These targets, propped in an infinite field, could be the exact end of all that light. Meanwhile, there is an unearthed tomb behind the bull's eye. A dead queen, her universe of jewels…

This to That and Thus

Right-handed? Use your left…
The first card, a man with a tarantula.
Then, from the left breast of Isis, blood.
Then, a lavender scarab, pinned
on a smock in a coffin.
Then, a bird of prey in Australia.
Then, a kite dropped from a bomber.
Then, meds for an associative disorder…
On the next card, I see a friend on a plane
who spontaneously aborts at 30,000 feet,
bleeds herself unconscious, awakes
in a city she has never heard of.
Then, weed killer in a shed.
Then, the repetition of a pattern
that mimics the delight of heaven.
Then, the cellophane dazzle of a dark
morning, & the words of Henry Vaughan:
Light is never so beautiful as in the presence of darkness.
Then, a stall wall defaming a dead singer.
Then, a boy with a galactic fighter —
the time warp is closing
A spooky void, end of a hall,
(go in there, the dream urges,
it's the room where your mother died.
Open your eyes, but look at nothing…)
Then, a light from beyond the sun.
Then, a magnitude missed in a heartbeat.
Then, boxcars, wheeling empty through a glade.
Then, a desert: *Now the last of my grief whitens and flakes.*
All that I was is now empty burning air…
Then, a transparent twin,
in bliss above the bed. The one
drowsing feels the shimmering light
pierce the drift of his unstrung love.
Then, island smoke, & a dungeon,

washed in lava. Only the prisoner lives.
Then, leaves the color of glass in a furnace.
Then, dubbed footage from Argentina,
a landmark snuff film, nothing but a hoax.
Then, the psychotropic allure of deadly fish.
Then, Judea goes dark. The sky splits wide.
Then, girls in gowns, barefoot on a beach.
Then, Central Park, the boathouse.
A wedding, Jewish. An old man lifts
his glass, looking out over the tables,
and at the bride and groom —
All this existed before the war,
in cities in Europe. And all of it is gone,
destroyed by devils set loose upon the world…
Then, parents mixing their blood
with warm water, pouring their
children a famine meal.
Then, a tripod on a porch,
lens bent to bits of foil in the sky.
Then, Halloween at a day care center —
a cat, a cave woman, a queen in a black veil.
Then, a branch, apple blossoms or tidal foam.
Then, the seething that cut the continents apart.
Then, I see you searching for the precedent
to all this. I see the history of heaven
opening at your touch, but showing
only foliage, fragrant water
spilling into four rivers, and fruit of
an orchard that exists only for pleasure…
In a dream, a mother is speaking to her children:
One Sunday walking home five years ago from church
I just went into the wrong house! I didn't die!
All this time, I've been right up the street,
wondering where you all were!
Then, an island. A green billow over
gray glitter. To the left of the deck, by
the pink marble bench, are three

beautiful women. A holiday
at the villa of the eldest. They are
the sad heirs of the fortune of the doctor
who wrote the textbook, the first in the field:
A Manual for the Management of Pain…
Then, your head has been
unscrewed at the neck. Don't be alarmed,
the witch says. These cards can be a lot like dreams.
The last card is a dream: your head's hollow
and metallic, you can—somehow —
look into it, there's a man with you
like a garage mechanic,
to nail down the cause of
the irritating rattle, that pebble
inside your hubcap. There it is:
a toy, a block, red & white, a letter
from the alphabet, carved on the side.

All the While

Some lie a day alone in bed
deciding that what they truly desire
is a briar tattoo around the upper arm.
Some look at a gutter in the rain and see
Anthony and Cleopatra adrift on a leaf.
Some pledge fidelity by a fountain…
Some see a link between lust
and the soul in the flames of flowers
or sunlit rain where blossoms drop in chunks.
Some drive to a concert in New Orleans,
some swear out restraining orders.
Some are deciding to be together
and some, not to be together.
And cells, microbes, chemicals,
and genes are deciding. The colors
of the crud show the decision
of the grains in the alchemist's bowl.
And regions, tribes, states and nations —
there are revolts and jubilees
and refugees on rafts,
kings hidden in bakery trucks.
There are sects and executions,
unlikely allies, unhappy homecomings…
Some smear aloe on each other
to recover what was once so magical
then a flash, rage ruins all between them.
Some spend time in online chat rooms.
Some recall the kiss of one who died
who lingers, just beyond the floodlight,
late evening, dew already forming…
Some decide a god is with them.
Some, no god is with them. Or a god
was once with them, but has left forever.
Some drink, thirsty as a lost soldier in a desert.
A green tint in the distance. The scent

of blossoming seems to reach him.
He can already taste what the trees
draw up from deep in the earth…
Some are conceiving others,
with difficulty, with ease, with both.
Some are deciding to leave this world.
Some would die horrible deaths all
over again to come back even if only
as a lower form of life, a spider
or a lizard on a tree at night.
Sky, torn corner of another world.
A future settles on the present.
Some chat over lunch and slowly
come to feel like they are talking in bed.
The steam table dissolves. The buzz of others
is a breeze that knocks the blinds against the sill.
Pale orange light of a lengthening afternoon
on the blinds, faces close. Perhaps
they will make love once more
before dressing for evening,
paella and wine, the feast
of Saint Objectivity.
Causes opt for fresh effects,
effects lay claim to new causes.
Some sidle next to others at parties.
Some meet in a motel by the boat basin.
In the dark of a puppet theater,
some doze, washed out
by a weekend in Terre Haute.
The hills are lush in a gold fog.
Some close their eyes during sex
 and see lights flashing. Others,
angst at bed's edge, condoms in trash:
That's how it is, you can get the fuck out…
The clouds are a shaped radiance.
Whatever comes to be, cries out in joy.
The male puppet has red whiskers

slashing at the woman puppet
with a long ugly blade.
She's in green, has braids,
wields a massive pair of shears.
Each takes turns decapitating the other.

Off the Map

Where the glacier covered
the road, one of us lit a cigarette
and envied the blue spin of the smoke.
*Please try a left. We haven't made a left
for days. I forget what a left is like...*
A petting zoo with wild coyotes.
A genocide skit in a state park
stragglers got as far as that grove...
There were many wrong turns.
In archaic faiths, verbal directions
at death get crucial. But who, now,
can follow anything not written down?
Our souls will circle some turnpike loop...
Overhead, the lightning is a glass arch.
The arch shatters. We cross into
a new world, the last in flames
at our heels. The radio
plays nothing but Sibelius.
Somewhere, a Kalevala Festival.
Somewhere the mountains are closed.
Somewhere the armies go home for the winter
& no one can say who rules the nation.
All this while we were talking about
the higher symmetry, then
the sordid end of a child star.
Motel mirrors are like movie props:
in one, we see a stop payment order.
In another, a cut phone line.
Later, one of us dreams a face,
beautiful, a half-eaten cherry between
a woman's pursed lips. The task
is not to kiss her, but take
in your lips the nibbled seed.
In the sink, the vortex is invisible.
Its shadow shines on the white basin

reminiscent of the sun during a full eclipse
a luminous black circle in a whitened sky…
Next turn, the Organ Donor Emporium.
Now might be time to look at a map.
The wild yellow lines breaking through
the boundary before shading into flame color
like the hair of a woman with a gas can
who has just burned down a library.
The airport, lost in a blizzard.
Next comes Jerusalem, or Paris,
or the Sahara. Camels crush the leaves.
The air fills with the scent of myrrh.
A medieval text says we are like
a bird flying though a mead hall at night.
From dark, back into the dark, for a few seconds
we feel warmth and glimpse the feasting —
There were insects all over me.
Out of my body, I could see my
own back stung to a welter.
I knew the garden was nearby.
In Kansas, it's another evening of
documentaries on millennial thought.
In Louisiana, men boil a caldron in a pit.
In Washington, lava slips down a hill.
In a painting by Francesco Clemente
a swimmer with sandbags tied to his limbs
rises against a slope of black ocean.
He will never break the surface.
But his lips press the apex
of the surging black wave, &
the turquoise universe and all
the stars fill his lungs.

www.ingramcontent.com/pod-product-compliance
Lightning Source LLC
Chambersburg PA
CBHW022114160426
43197CB00009B/1024